# TOKYO

## City on the edge

Todd Crowell & Stephanie Forman Morimura

**ASIA 2000**

An Orchid Pavilion Book
Asia 2000 Limited
Hong Kong

ISBN: 962–7160–80–6


Published by Asia 2000 Ltd
Fifth Floor, 31A Wyndham Street
Central, Hong Kong

http://www.asia2000.com.hk


Typeset in Goudy by Asia 2000 Ltd
Printed in Hong Kong by Editions Quaille


First Printing 2002

For Setsuko

For Kenji, a master of the art of *gamman*,
who was there every step of the way

—

# Contents

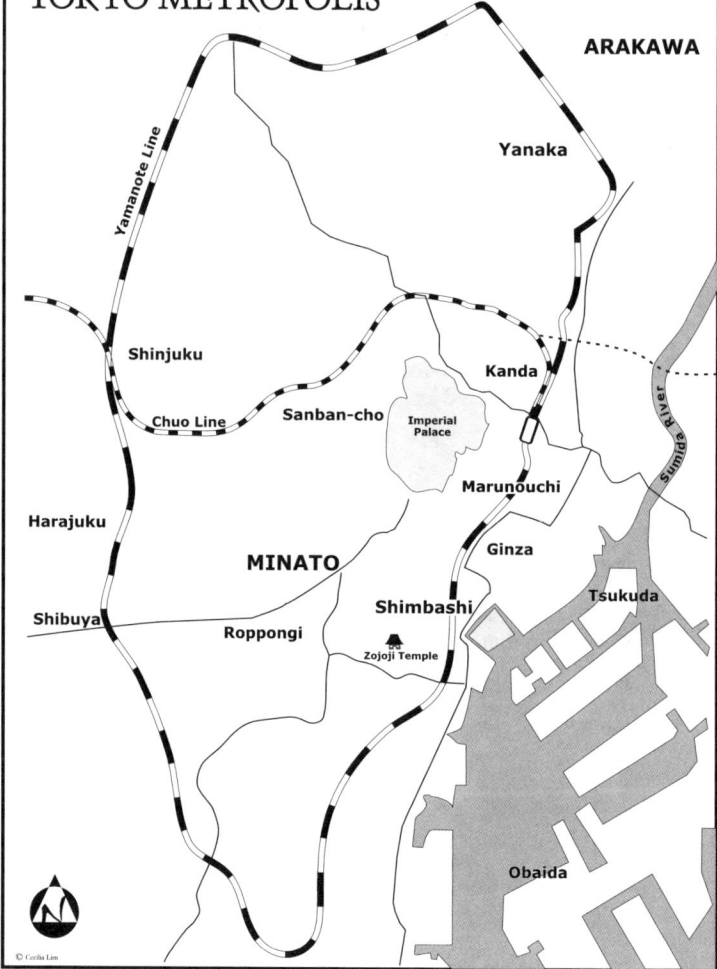

# TOKYO METROPOLIS

**ARAKAWA**

Yanaka

Yamanote Line

Shinjuku

Kanda

Chuo Line

Sanban-cho

Imperial Palace

Marunouchi

Harajuku

**MINATO**

Ginza

Shibuya

Roppongi

Shimbashi

Zojoji Temple

**Tsukuda**

Sumida River

Obaida

© Cecilia Lim

# Prologue

I could feel the tremor, gentle at first, then quickly growing stronger and stronger. Suddenly, I was being jerked from side to side by a violent motion. I scrambled under the kitchen table, my head bumping against the top as I tried to fit my bulk under it. The movement was now truly intense, like an airliner in the worst imaginable turbulence. I heard a shriek. From terror or excitement? Mercifully, the tremor began to subside. Then from outside I heard a voice saying, "*mo ikkai*" one more time. And the furious shaking began again, jerking and swaying, jerking and swaying.

Somewhat shakily, I climbed down from the earthquake simulator. It was a small box made up to look like a typical Japanese kitchen, and it rested on top of a flatbed truck belonging to the Tokyo Metropolitan Police. The room was connected to a machine that simulated a violent earthquake, moving rapidly from two to seven on the Japan Meteorological Agency scale. In a quake measured at seven, the agency says, "over 30 percent of the houses will collapse, landslides will occur, ground cracks and fractures will open in the earth's crust."

September 1 is officially designated Disaster Prevention Day to commemorate the Great Kanto Earthquake, which hit Tokyo at exactly two minutes before noon on that day in 1923. It also prepares people for a repeat, which everyone knows will happen sooner or later. It was reported that 12 million citizens of central Japan took part in this day's disaster drill. The newspapers showed the Prime Minister dressed in fatigues and chatting with a nurse at a drill in Kawasaki. A Japanese naval vessel simulated the unloading of food for 100,000 refugees in Shimizu, south of the capital. Although the newspapers reported that large numbers of people participated in these events, the editorial writers bemoaned the falling interest in such drills and a growing complacency. Perhaps they should have. The Great Kanto Earthquake, named after the vast plain on central Honshu Island, is Japan's greatest disaster. About 140,000 people were crushed, burned or drowned in the quake and in the massive fires that followed.

The devastation wrought by the earthquake and by the American air force fire-bombings in late World War II was to have profound and long-lasting consequences for the development of Tokyo. They destroyed almost all vestiges of old Edo, which is why no private and few public buildings or monuments dating from as near as the Meiji Period (1868-1912) remain and why the preservation ethic in Tokyo is weak, compared with many other cities. The disasters hastened the movement of people to the western parts and suburbs along the rapidly expanding network of private rail lines. And it spawned another Tokyo phenomenon, a fondness for grandiose plans for the rebuilding and remaking of Tokyo along fantastic new lines. Most of them come to naught because of the sheer expense.

The day after the drill, the Tokyo Metropolitan Government released another estimate of the casualties an earthquake of the same destructive force would cause. The Great Kanto Earthquake, with its epicenter in Sagami Bay, south of Tokyo, registered 7.9 on the Richter Scale. About 3 percent of the buildings would be destroyed, 40 percent of the people made homeless and 9,400 people killed. But it is only one estimate. Others estimate much higher casualties. In 1988, the National Land Agency estimated deaths as perhaps as high as 150,000. Tokyo is the largest city in the world today, but it is the only one with an indeterminate death sentence hanging over it.

Some years ago, a geology professor named Hiroshi Kawasumi made popular the notion that big earthquakes occur in the Tokyo area on the average of once every 69 years. He based this theory on a detailed study of recurring quakes going back to the year 818. If he is right, then Tokyo is well over-due for another one. Fortunately, the 69-year theory is widely dismissed by experts, who believe that the science behind it is faulty. Somewhat more credence is given to scientist Katsuhiko Ishibashi's "72-year" theory, based on the cycle of major earthquakes occurring near the town of Odawara, close to Tokyo. Since the last one was the Great Kanto Earthquake itself, that would mean that the next quake — the Big One as everyone calls it — is due anytime.

But there is one seismic theory in which scientists in Japan place considerable faith. This is the theory that a quake of the magnitude of 8 on the Richter Scale is due to hit the coast of Japan off Suruga Bay at any time. This is where three of the world's largest tectonic plates rub together: the Eurasian Plate, the Philippine Sea Plate and the massive Pacific Plate. An earthquake of magnitude 8 would surely cause tremendous damage in Tokyo, too. The last Big One occurred in Suruga Bay in 1854, and records show that it recurs every 100-150 years. This theory is buttressed by modern geological theories concerning plate movements and physical evidence of land subsiding in the region. Most of the country's considerable investment in earthquake prediction is directed at predicting this cataclysm, known as the Tokai Earthquake.

The Chinese were the first to correctly predict a major earthquake in time to evacuate a city. They saved about 100,000 people in Haicheng in Manchuria from the consequences of a 7.3 scale quake. Yet a year later they failed utterly to forecast the quake that leveled Tanshan, killing at least 250,000. The San Andreas Fault in California is packed with sensors and other prediction paraphernalia in what has been described as the world's largest experiment in earthquake prediction. But it is not integrated into a specific evacuation or warning plan. Japan has the only scheme designed to predict a quake in time for people to take precautions.

To find out how, I visited the National Earthquake Prediction Center, located near the northeast end of the Imperial Palace. This is not a laboratory. It is an operational facility. Its mission, simply put, is to predict the next Big One — not to mention little ones, volcanic eruptions and tsunamis — in time to warn the public. I took my shoes off as I entered the center. Two technicians were on duty monitoring rows of seismographs and computers. At least 1,000 tremors large enough to be felt occur in the Japanese archipelago every year, so one might reasonably expect some activity. Sure enough, on one of the machines a stylo was tracing small blue arcs on a roll of grid paper. Somewhere in Ibaraki prefecture north of the capital, an earthquake was in progress, but we in this room were probably the only people who knew about it. "It's too small to be felt," said my guide, Noritake Nishide, Assistant Director of the Management Division of the Japan Meteorological Agency's Seismological and Volcanology Department.

On the wall was a large map of Japan, showing the location of the more than 100 seismographs and other sensors that feed data into this room constantly. Most of them measure ground movements, but there are other instruments, such as strain meters, which are at the bottom of deep wells and measure changes in bedrock pressure and water-filled tubes called tilt meters that measure the attitude of the landscape. Nishide believes that the Big One likely would be presaged by a series of smaller tremors and the rise of a few millimeters of land elevations. "If they [the tremors] reached the point of ten small quakes in an hour, at least three of them being at 4 on the Richter Scale, a committee of scientists would convene." Known formally as the Earthquake Assessment Committee, it is universally referred to as the six "wise men." Alerted by pagers, they would be whisked to the prediction center, where they would evaluate the data and advise the prime minister whether to issue a public warning.

Nishide showed me the room where the six "wise men" would meet to deliberate. It is functional in layout. Along the walls are more computers, and at one side is an oblong table where the wise men would gather. In one corner is a fax machine with a dedicated line to the Prime Minister's office. A partition in the hallway ceiling can be lowered to seal off the room from the frightened masses, who might descend on the building if word leaked that the committee was meeting to decide whether to issue a warning.

If the prime minister were to make an announcement, it would, according to the Tokyo Metropolitan Police pamphlet, *Earthquake Precautions*, go something like this: "A big earthquake is expected to occur very soon (within a period of several hours or two to three days, depending on the warning). Everyone should prepare for disaster." People would then react calmly and rationally, or so one hopes. Some years ago, shortly after the prediction system was established, somebody in the small town of Hiratsuka near Tokyo mistakenly played the prerecorded tape over loudspeakers with the mayor's warning that the Big One was coming. Telephone calls flooded the city hall switchboard asking what was going on and what to do. Of course, another possibility exists, namely that most people would simply ignore the warning.

All of this instrumentation looks impressive, but there is one gaping hole in Japan's earthquake-prediction system: Tokyo. In the great conurbation of 30 million people, there are too many noises to read and interpret the instruments properly. Although a few sensors have been buried very deep beneath the city, there are none at intermediate levels to help warn of shallow quakes. The prediction system is set up basically to warn people of a return of the Tokai Earthquake, not the Great Kanto Earthquake. "There aren't enough instruments, and the conditions are very bad," laments Nishide. "We think it is possible to predict the next Tokai earthquake," he says referring to the one expected off Suruga Bay. "It is considered much more difficult, possibly impossible given the current state of warning technology, to predict the next Kanto quake with any precision," he said. Fortunately, he and other scientists think it may still be a long way off, 69-year theories notwithstanding, giving them more time to refine their techniques.

Some believe that the whole exercise is a waste of time, and that the approximately $100 million that the government spends on earthquake prediction each year could be better spent on other things. They note that for all of this effort, the system failed to predict the Great Hanshin Earthquake that centered on Kobe in 1995. To be fair, not much attention or effort is devoted to predicting quakes in the Kansai region. American experts in particular believe that prediction is near impossible. None of the so-called precursors, they argue, has ever been shown to be a reliable indicator of an impending quake. But the Japanese remain believers. The five-year prediction program which expired in 1999 was replaced by another one.

In the eastern part of Tokyo, in a small park in the Sumida ward, just north of where the giant wrestlers cause the earth to tremble when they collide in the ring of the national sumo stadium, is a memorial to the victims of the Great Kanto Earthquake. It is also dedicated to victims of America's fire-bombing attacks in March 1945 which devastated the same part of the city and killed about as many people. In the center is a three-tier pagoda made of concrete, which shelters the remains of the victims in large urns. Attached to it is a large memorial hall ringed with paintings of the tragedy. Many are rather gruesome. In one a priest was praying over a mound of skulls. When I visited, it was the anniversary of the quake and the grounds were crowded. Monks in white and yellow robes were chanting and beating drums. Many people, mostly middle-aged or elderly, approached the temple to place flowers in a large urn along with scraps of paper with prayers on them. At one end of the hall, there was a string of a thousand paper cranes, a Japanese symbol of hope.

Off to one side of the memorial building is a polished granite monument honoring Koreans living in Japan who were killed following the quake. It looks a lot newer than the other monuments here, a belated recognition of one aspect of the disaster that many Japanese would like to forget. Thousands of Koreans died on those hot September days, but they weren't crushed in buildings or burned in fires. They were killed by roving bands of crazed Japanese, who had heard and were apparently all too willing to believe rumors that the Koreans were poisoning wells. The pogrom lasted several days. Ethnic Koreans living in Japan are less inclined these days to let their fellow countrymen forget such incidents. At a small booth they were selling books about the tragedy. Yet there was a feeling of reconciliation, too. A Korean and a Japanese Buddhist priest exchanged friendly words.

A festive air prevailed on the warm September day. Balloons were flying, and stalls were selling *yakitori*, the popular skewered chicken snack. Along a lane, people in booths demonstrated first-aid techniques and sold survival supplies. The earthquake simulator was a big attraction with children, who seemed to view it as a kind of a amusement park ride. At one side of the park, young women in gay kimonos were practicing the tea ceremony. Even so, this is a sad place, poignant with memories. It was within these small confines, no larger than a supermarket parking lot, that the greatest tragedy occurred. Most of the destruction was caused by fire. The 1923 quake happened as thousands of housewives were preparing the noon meal. Cooking pots tipped over or were abandoned, setting off a conflagration that raged for three-days. That's the legend, anyway. The fire was probably accelerated by chemicals, gasoline and electric wires, too. People fled their burning and crumbling houses and sought refuge in open spaces, of which there were precious few then and not that many more today.

Many headed for vacant ground that recently had housed an army clothing depot. By mid-afternoon, some 40,000 people had crowded in, but fires converged on them from three directions. A superheated vacuum formed in the air above and drew the flames closer and closer, pumping up the winds and creating cyclones. British geologist and writer Peter Hadfield describes what happened next in his book **Sixty Seconds That will Change the World**: "As the sun sank, and darkness fell, the thousands trapped in the depot realized to their horror their predicament and likely fate. A hot burning cyclone emerged from the wall of flame and swept across the ground, raining ash and cinders on the screaming multitude. More cyclones followed, terrifying spirals of fire that sucked people up and out of the crowds and dropped them in balls of fire. In one indescribable holocaust all but a few hundred of the tens of thousands who had sought refuge in the depot perished." Only a few dozen meters away is the Sumida River, and it must have seemed like succor. It was, in fact, another death trap. Most of the bridges that then spanned the river were still made of wood, and they caught fire like everything else and then collapsed under the weight of the people. Possibly more people drowned in the Great Kanto Earthquake than were crushed in falling buildings.

I have been to the Peace Garden Park in Hiroshima, which is, of course, dedicated to the atomic bombing of the city. That shrine is much better known than this Memorial Temple to the Two Great Disasters, even though the death tolls from the Hiroshima-Nagasaki bombings and the quake-fire bombings were comparable. One gets the impression that few foreigners venture here. None of the exhibits in the memorial temple museum, filled with things like charred violins and clocks with their hands forever stuck on noon, has English subtitles. There were no other foreigners I could notice with me at the memorial. At Hiroshima, the motto could be "Never again," and it is possible in this day to believe that things like nuclear weapons are amenable to human controls. The sadness of this place lies in the knowledge that no one can say "Never again." The forces of nature that are moving inexorably towards another catastrophe are impervious to human intervention. Someday — next year, twenty years or 200 years from now — the pressures building up will finally snap. Meanwhile, the great city can only watch . . . and wait.

— T.C.

# 1

# Viewpoints

Tokyo makes a lousy first impression. Maybe it has something to do with the way most visitors see the place for the first time. The international airport at Narita is located far out in the countryside. Aircraft approach the single runway over rice paddies, denying the passenger the momentary thrill of seeing the great city spread out beneath him. The traveler then stumbles bleary-eyed from a flight into the arrival hall of the "New" Tokyo International Airport Terminal One, which, though built in the early 1970s, was until its recent renovation, beginning to look dingy and disorganized, especially compared with the sleek and efficient new portals in Singapore and Hong Kong. Signs are not clearly posted, people and their fully loaded luggage carts block the way; everywhere is a distinct overlay of stale cigarette smoke.

And the arrival at Narita is not the end of the journey. Another commute is required to actually get into the city. Only two means are practical: train or limousine bus, since a taxi ride would bankrupt an Arab prince. Most people will probably take the bus, which is still the most convenient way to make the long trek. This means stuffing the tired body into another narrow seat, designed, it seems, with the average body size of the pre-war Japanese in mind. There is even less legroom than the most crowded airplane economy cabin. Returning locals, knowing they still have a two-hour journey left, promptly fall asleep. The excited newcomer, momentarily forgetting the discomfort, stares through the window, wondering when he is ever going to get a glimpse of the destination. The first hour presents little more to see than rice fields and farm houses with black-tiled roofs — Japan to be sure, but where does Tokyo begin?

He or she looks in vain for a landmark, maybe nothing like the dramatic skyline of New York or Hong Kong but at least some unique feature, something like the dome of Sacre Coeur Cathedral atop Montmartre in Paris that lets the traveller know that he has arrived. In fact, the first recognizable feature, after about an hour and a half of riding through rice fields, is the fairy tale castle rising out of the expanse of Tokyo Disneyland, which strictly speaking is not even in Tokyo. From that spot, the city begins to encroach rapidly, if not dramatically. The bus crosses the Arakawa River and heads into the downtown. From the elevated highway the rider peers into the windows of office warrens filled with the fabled Japanese salarymen hunched over their desks. Soon thereafter, the airport bus finally pulls up at one of the hotels in West Shinjuku.

Tokyo is just not a city that can be seen from above or from a distance. A first time visitor might wander to the towering Tokyo City Hall Offices and ride the elevator to the observation platform on the 48th floor. The vast city stretches out as far as the eye can see in all directions, a gray ocean of nondescript, box-like buildings. The viewer searches for a pattern or some kind of discernible feature — that patch of green, the grounds of the Imperial Palace, in the distance the rust red spire of Tokyo Tower, a copy of the one in Paris. But nothing seems to stand out and nothing prepares the traveler for that inevitable moment when he will be asked by some Japanese, "what's your impression of Tokyo?" He searches desperately for something polite to say, usually coming up with a vacuous, "It's certainly big," or "It's crowded." If one really threw caution to the wind, one might admit it is ugly. That would probably elicit not an angry response but a knowing smile.

The city hides its considerable charms, and it takes some time to uncover them. Tokyo has been described a thousand times as a collection of villages. And it is within these villages, each with a small-town ambience, that Tokyo's real heart is to be found. Here are pleasant residential neighborhoods fronting narrow, unnamed streets, full of surprisingly spacious houses surrounded by flowers and bonsai trees and small shops selling wooden sandals or tatami mats that somehow still survive despite the rapidly encroaching Starbucks, Gaps, and Dunkin' Donuts. Once filled with drab, ferro-concrete buildings erected in the poverty of the post-war years, Tokyo is breaking out with splashy new buildings, replete with strange arches, colors and crazy angles. The city's weekly what's-on magazine is a centimeter thick and packed with things to do. On any given weekend, 100 popular or classical music shows and an equal number of plays, operas and ballets may be on the boards. Tokyo boasts the world's largest indoor ski run and museums for every taste.

But Tokyo is also a city that works. More than 20 private rail lines, not counting a dozen subway lines, criss-cross the metropolis moving millions of people every day, not always in comfort but always on time. The streets are immaculate, and ordinary street crime is so rare that people still often leave their front doors unlocked. The various municipal subdivisions pamper their constituents. They provide sign-language interpreters for the deaf, home helpers for the elderly, subsidies both for single-family households and to encourage young people to have children. Sometimes the local government can get a little too intrusive. People are required to separate their trash into collectible recyclables and nonrecyclables and to put all household garbage in specially produced transparent bags that do not pollute during incineration. Still, the city produces millions of tons of trash a year, peaking at 4.9 million tons in 1989, and landfill space in Tokyo Bay is running out.

Of the world's 500 largest companies, about 100 have their head offices in Tokyo. London and New York boast about 50 each. More than half of the Japanese firms with capitalization of ¥5 trillion or more are based in the capital. Those companies that continue to maintain their head offices in the provinces maintain such large Tokyo branches that they might as well be based there. Toshiba, Nissan Motor Co., and Fuji Film are but three of the many Japanese manufacturing giants that have moved to Tokyo in recent years. Those large corporations that continue to hold out in the smaller cities, Toyota near Nagoya and Matsushita Electric Corp. in Osaka, for example, now seem almost eccentric. Only a few minutes from Tokyo Station is a no-frills hotel that is often called the "MEI dormitory" because so many businessmen who stay there are men from Matsushita visiting the capital on business.

Before the 1980s, Tokyo's contribution to the country's economic output was relatively constant at 15 percent. Now it is closer to 20 percent. About a quarter of Japan's more than 400,000 factories are located here, but it is in the service industries where new products are conceived, designed and incubated, that Tokyo's real dominance is most evident. Nearly half of the country's research institutes are located here, 40 percent of its information companies and 30 percent of its new ventures. Almost all of the country's elite universities are concentrated in and around the capital, and 70 percent of their graduates stay to take jobs here. Tokyo is home for nearly half of Japan's writers, 47 percent of its accountants, 52 percent of its computer software writers, and most of its television broadcasters. In 1992, Tokyo surpassed New York as the world's advertising capital with $24.5 billion in annual billings. Metropolitan Tokyo area produces goods and services valued at some $565 billion. The city budget of $50 billion exceeds the national budget of most countries. If it were an independent country, its gross domestic product would rank about the size of Canada's. Put another way, the people here generate about 2 percent of the world's gross domestic product, and they do it with only 0.6 percent of the world's population living on .0001 percent of its surface.

Tokyo has been largest city in the world since at least the 18th century. It had more than a million residents when London had only about 850,000. Despite fire, war and disaster, the population has never fallen below a million inhabitants. Setting an exact population figure for Tokyo today, however, is a matter of definition. The historic subdivisions of old Tokyo, known as *ku* have been fixed at 23 since 1947. "Ku" is usually translated into English as "ward," but this is misleading since they are more than electoral districts. They function more like boroughs in New York City or London. Residents elect their own council and chief executive (who usually styles himself as "mayor" in English). Thus the "ward area" of Tokyo has about 8 million people. But the Governor of Tokyo presides over a larger domain, Tokyo Prefecture, which is akin to a state or province. The actual city of Tokyo was abolished as a war measure in 1943. Tokyo prefecture, or *Tokyo To* in Japanese, extends about 100 km into the interior, embracing such large suburban cities as Musashino, Tachikawa and Hachioji as well as 23 other smaller cities, five towns and one village. Also included are a number of offshore islands in the Pacific Ocean. The population of Tokyo prefecture is about 12 million.

Still, Tokyo does not stop where politicians draw the political boundaries. Anyone crossing into neighboring Kanagawa or Chiba prefectures would not feel he is entering the countryside. Thus, metropolitan Tokyo sprawls out to engulf more cities along the edge of Tokyo Bay and toward the mountains in the interior. This includes the city of Yokohama, which, with more than 3 million residents, is actually the country's second-largest city with a proud history all its own. It crosses into Saitama prefecture and parts of Ibaraki and moves into the edges of Yamanashi. This is known as the National Capital Region with Tokyo as its hub. It has a population of some 31,610,000 people, the largest concentration of humanity on the planet.

When Tokyo compares itself with other cities, it finds few peers. Population isn't the only criterion. Mexico City or greater Sao Paulo may be approaching Tokyo in terms of sheer numbers. Seoul with some 10 million has more people than the 23 wards. But when Tokyo looks for equals, it sees only London, New York and perhaps Paris. Only these and Tokyo form a select group of "world cities" which, in terms of population, economic power and such intangibles as culture, can be considered among the truly elite. The Tokyo Metropolitan Government first described itself as a "world city" in the Second Long Term Plan published in 1986. It said that, "in the 21st Century Tokyo will grow into a city with 12 million people, an active city with many generations helping each other, a pleasant city with lots of greenery, water, information centers and one of the biggest bases of the world economy, a city that balances businesses with residences. Such a city will be an international city that will lead the world. It would be the World City, Tokyo."

Tokyo is not just a "world city;" in some ways it was already a 21st century city even before the turn of the century. The city is dotted with projects that proclaim themselves to be the "futuristic city of the 21st century." But then Tokyo has often stimulated the imagination of writers or filmmakers searching for a metaphor for the future. When the late Russian film director Andrei Tarkovsky needed images of a city on a distant planet for his look-to-the-future movie *Solaris* (1977), he found them in Tokyo's then new expressways. His hero driving aimlessly along them was meant to express the absurdity of the new world he had encountered. Presumably, Tarkovsky never got caught in Tokyo traffic. It is hardly surprising that cyberpunk author William Gibson choose Tokyo as the setting for his futuristic novels, such as *Idoru*. And American movie director Ridley Scott was inspired by Shinjuku's skyline to create a 21st century Los Angeles for his 1982 film noir, *Blade Runner*. Harrison Ford chases renegade robots against a backdrop of neon and high-rise buildings. One hears echoes in the robotic voices that welcome one into the department stores.

Nobody ever accused Tokyoites of dwelling in the past. Change has truly been the only constant. Fires, earthquakes and bombs have over the years completely destroyed major parts of the city, leaving a sense of impermanence. When things do burn down or are otherwise destroyed, they are either rebuilt as they were, like most of the major temples and shrines of the city, or something entirely different takes its place, leaving behind no indication of what was once there. Almost nothing authentic remains of the Tokyo of a time as recent as the 19th century. Anything "old" is usually no older than the Taisho Period, named after the current emperor's grandfather, which merely goes back to the 1920s. Anyone wanting to get the feel of old Edo, as the nation's capital was called from the 15th until the 19th centuries, must turn to museums and theme parks. Sometimes echoes of the past exist in place names, such as the Toranomon district, where the American Embassy is located. Toranomon translates as the "Tiger Gate", and is a reminder that the outer grounds of the shogun's palace used to extend beyond the boundaries of the present-day Imperial Palace grounds.

The preservation ethic is weak. The owners of the old Imperial Hotel, a Tokyo landmark designed by American architect Frank Lloyd Wright, bulldozed it so they could build a taller and more profitable structure, despite an international hue and cry. The original lobby of the Imperial Hotel was moved to a theme park near Nagoya; the rest of the structure was demolished in 1968. The only other remaining Frank Lloyd Wright building in Tokyo is the Myonichikan built in 1921 and located in the Ikebukuro district. It was built for the Jiyu Gakuen, or Freedom School, a pioneer establishment in progressive education in Japan and has fared better than the hotel. It has been listed as a historical building. Aficionados were unable to save the venerable Tokiwa-za Theater, the heart of Asakusa's old entertainment district, which was demolished to make space for another nondescript hotel. Occasionally, one landmark or another may escape the wrecker's ball, for Japanese do possess a certain sentimentality for old buildings but only if they don't stand in the way of progress or profits. So far, residents of Ueno have successfully prevented the construction of an underground parking lot under Shinobazu Pond, beloved of old woodblock prints. It is thought that a parking lot might drain the pond.

The most important recent event in the lives of most Tokyoites was a man-made disaster. Almost everyone was affected in one way or other by the extraordinary buildup in asset prices of the late 1980s, which the Japanese now call the "Bubble Era." In many ways it was as defining a time for Tokyo as Paris in the '20s or New York in the

'50s. Its subsequent collapse beginning in 1990 gave everyone in Tokyo, and of course in Japan, a severe hangover from which they are still recovering. Ordinary people found that the humble family estate had made them millionaires on paper, only to feel like paupers as property prices fell in the post-Bubble recession or if they were forced to sell to pay the inheritance taxes. Of course, hordes of bankers, developers and other intermediaries were only too happy to help them through their plight, so that, quick as a flash, the family home, even on the tiniest of lots, could turn into a new office complex or apartment building. As the recession continues and major institutions are brought down one after another, Tokyoites, especially baby boomers, are seeing the landscape shift even more. Officials at the most elite of government agencies, the Ministry of Finance, were arrested. CEOs of firms thought to be as permanent as Mt. Fuji were seen sobbing at press conferences announcing the demise of the company. The birth rate is dropping, population is ageing and the government is pressed for money.

So at the end of the 20th century, change is once again afoot. The news is full of end time. The last Morse Code station in Japan closed. A department store in the Nihonbashi district, which opened more than 330 years ago and was the first Japanese store to allow customers to enter with their shoes on and the first to install an elevator, closed. A notice posted on the closed shutter of the Sakuraya camera shop, whose huge neon sign marked Shinjuku Station's East Exit for as long as anyone can remember, announces that the shop has shut its doors forever. The look of shock and bewilderment on the faces of passersby says it all: "Et tu, Sakuraya?"

# 2

# Movement

The station platform begins filling up early at Musashi-sakai on the Chuo railway line west of Tokyo. Most of the passengers are men dressed in conservative suits. They flash their monthly passes and descend the concrete steps to the platform. It's 7:30 a.m., but the trains are already crowded. It is impossible to find a seat, so most of the passengers are resigned to making the trip into the capital standing up, one hand threaded through the plastic strap overhead. The lucky few who occupy the benches have fallen asleep again, their heads drooping down into their chests. Or, they have their faces buried in *manga* comic books, or newspapers. Some of those standing up are reading, being careful to fold the newspaper into eighths so that they don't jab their neighbors in the ribs with their elbows. It is an art form, like origami. Most are already standing so close to each other that they are almost touching.

Many will change trains at Shinjuku Station, Tokyo's busiest portal. Some two and a half million passengers converge here every day from 20 different railway and subway lines to catch one of the

3,000 daily departures. Here the platform isn't just crowded. Virtually every square meter of space is occupied. Platoons of station attendants do their best to carve out pathways in this sea of humanity so that those disembarking from the on-coming train can get out of the car. Even before the last person alights, there is a surge toward the doors. The last few enter backwards, wiggling their bodies as they wedge themselves in just enough for the car doors to close. Some people boldly thrust themselves into the mass; others try to slip in from the side. Those wanting to read manuver close to the door, where they might find a modicum of space. Others, anxious to get out at the right station and worried about having to fight their way through the mob favor the last-in, first-out method, waiting to enter just as the doors close. The experienced commuter chooses which car to enter with care. He knows when to ride in the front of the train, when to ride in the back, or when to ride in, say, the third car from the front. Arriving just at the desired subway exit can cut down on walking time, especially at massive stations, like the Otemachi Station, that sprawl for miles. As a rule, the best seat, if one is lucky enough to get a seat, is the one at the end of the row. If it becomes vacant, people shuffle down to sit on it, even if they happen to be sitting in the very next space.

Now the bodies are not merely brushing against each other. They are crushed together. Faces are jammed against the windows, features distorted against the glass. The car is air-conditioned, but necks still drip with perspiration. In winter, heavy overcoats make the train car feel even more crowded. There is no real need to hold on to the over-head strap. Nobody could possibly fall over now. Even if you let go of your briefcase, it would not fall to the floor. As the train slows to stop at another station, people lodged in the middle of the car claw their way toward the exit, panicky that they might not be able to get out in the few seconds before the doors snap shut and the train moves on. Apologies are mumbled as elbows gouge ribs and toes are trampled. A woman grimaces, as she is jammed painfully against an upright pole by the crush of bodies.

The trip back to the suburbs in the evening is not usually so frantic, but then the commuters are more tired. Many businessmen stay at their desks until 7 p.m. or later. Once or twice a week comes the obligatory after-hours drinking session with colleagues in a restaurant or nightclub. Thus, many of the late-night passengers have a kind of glazed look. One or two may be mumbling a sentimental song they had sung at a party earlier in the evening. Late at night the atmosphere inside the cars smells faintly of alcohol. The drunks come in many styles: a middle-aged man red in the face slumps on a seat loudly snoring; a youth gets sick in a corner; and another hangs with his hand looped through the overhead strap, his body limp. American writer Donald Richie, a longtime resident of the city, has written: "There is nothing wearier-looking than a weary Tokyoite. Alertness temporarily suppressed, he falls asleep on the subway, even slumbers standing up, yet he manages to stumble out at his stop."

The trains do not run 24-hours a day. Midnight is the witching hour, and an unholy scramble ensues to catch the last train home. People who have missed it rush about frantically waving their arms to flag down a taxi, many of which seem to have "reserved" or "out-of-service" signs on their dash boards. Or, they join a taxi line that might be 50-people deep, the last person having to wait perhaps an hour before catching a ride. The hours between midnight and 2 a.m. are the golden hours for Tokyo's taxi drivers, most of whom angle to pick up long hauls to the far suburbs that can earn them a fare of $100 or more. Some men give up and book a night in a capsule hotel, which might be considerably cheaper than hiring a cab for the long ride home. The last train on the Chuo line departs Tokyo Station at

12:18 a.m., and it finally comes to rest at Takao Station at 1:37 a.m. Then the system is quiet for a few hours, until 4:29 a.m., when the first train pulls out of Takao, and the madness starts over again.

Most of the residents of this city spend at least three hours of their day undergoing *tsukin jigoku*, or commuting hell. But round trips lasting four hours or more are by no means unusual. That elusive but very desirable thing called an affordable house has proven to be a moveable object. In 1965, it could be found in Ogikubo, only about ten minutes from Shinjuku on the Chuo line. A decade later, it had migrated as far away as Tachikawa. And by 1990, it had moved out of Tokyo altogether, coming to rest in Yamanashi prefecture, more than 60 km away from the city center. Whenever the newspapers or magazines are hard up for a story, they often try to find the commuter with the longest trip to make and describe his daily trial. By common agreement, the King of the Commuters has been Tadao Masuda. For nearly 25 years, he spent nearly six and a half hours travelling to and from his home in Mito, 130 km north of Tokyo, to Yokohama where he worked. It cost him about $600 in train fares alone each month. Masuda rose at 4:30 a.m., breakfasted and arrived at Mito station to catch the 5:33 a.m. train. He pulled into Yokohama at 8:23 a.m. During his more than three-hour ride, he changed trains three times, skillfully navigating such notorious commuter hell-holes as Ueno-Okachimachi Station. Masuda said he did not want to take a convenience apartment closer to his office, as some salarymen do, because he did not want to be apart from his family. By the time he got home in the evening, he says, he had already forgotten the worries of the office.

Commuting by train is the quintessential experience of the Tokyo native. Perhaps a few company presidents are driven to work in a company car; some others brave the traffic by driving into the city in their own cars on one of the expressways. Everyone else rides the crowded commuter trains. Bar hostesses and company vice presidents stand together in wretched equality. There can be few more levelling experiences. In the greater Tokyo area, about 20 million people use the trains every day — about two-thirds of the population. Of course, other major cities have their own commuter trains, subways and traffic jams, but nowhere else does the simple act of getting to work seem to be such a defining experience. In Tokyo, the commuter train has taken on legendary, even epic proportions. With horrified fascination, the outside world watches the Tokyoites' daily ordeal. Images of crowded railroad stations and uniformed "pushers" shoving bodies into the cars have been staples of nearly every published account of the city at least since the Tokyo Olympic Games in 1964.

The average Tokyo commuter car is sometimes packed to 210 percent of its rated capacity at rush hour. This is actually an improvement. In the late 1960s, the average was more like 260 percent. The Ministry of Transportation is quite specific about what these figures mean. At 150 percent capacity, it says, "shoulders touch, but passengers can still comfortably read a newspaper." At 200 percent, "the bodies are firmly pressed together, making it impossible to read a newspaper but magazines can still be read." At 250 percent, "you can't move your arms or feet. When the train suddenly changes speed, riders find themselves thrown off balance." At 300 percent the ride is "physically almost impossible and dangerous!" As part of a grand design to make Japan a "lifestyle superpower", the national government has made it official policy that this capacity figure be brought down to an average of 180 percent. Meanwhile, the average in London, Paris and New York is a little more than 100 percent.

Tokyo train cars are considerably smaller than those in other major cities, which is one reason why they are so crowded. The floor area of a typical car is about 50 square meters, compared with 75 square meters in London. A New York subway car has seats for 144 people, and a London car seats about 100. But a typical 154-passenger car in Tokyo has places for only 54 people to sit down. Thus, even when it is filled to merely 100 percent capacity, there will be nearly twice as many people standing as sitting. A London car filled to 100 percent capacity would have about 100 people sitting and 10 to 35 people standing. Subway cars in inner London do have fewer seats, but the ride is usually shorter. In Tokyo the trains from the suburbs to downtown are no different in size, and people often have to ride standing up all of the way.

For the most part, the dimensions of the railway cars have not changed since pre-war years. Of course, for many years, Japan's railroads were state monopolies, with all of the featherbedding and inertia that that implies. In the 1980s, however, the lines were broken up and privatized, introducing an element of competition and some spirit of innovation and customer service. All of the coaches on Acty, the newest highspeed train on the JR Tokaido line, for example, are double-decked, which gives commuters a better chance of finding a seat. It is a special boon for many people making the long commute into Tokyo from Shizuoka and Kanagawa prefectures in the west. The Tokyo Waterfront New Transport Inc., created to serve the new city center planned on reclaimed land in Tokyo Bay, runs a new computer-controlled monorail train that runs on rubber tires but on its own tracks, a kind of hybrid train-bus but one that arrives and departs on more precise schedules.

Automated ticketing is now universal, making the once familiar ticket-taker, with his ticket punch clicking incessantly, a figure from history. Passengers glide through the turnstiles, putting the ticket in the slot and smoothly retrieving it at the end. Standing in front and fumbling around in the pocket for a ticket is a definite no-no. During the rush hour, even a second's hesitation can turn the pathway into a bottleneck. The stations themselves are often unattractive compared with the newer and sleeker underground stations in Singapore, Washington or Moscow. Some of the downtown stations now have escalators, but for the most part passengers have to scramble up and down hard concrete steps to get to the train platforms. There are relatively few accommodations for handicapped people. Those in wheel chairs are carried up and down stairs by station attendants, and they complain that the doors into the comfort rooms are too narrow to get through. To try to humanize their stations, the JR East replaced the klaxons that announced train departures with light, relaxing music. Yamaha Corp., makers of the famous piano, was commissioned to write special signature tunes for Shinjuku, Shibuya and some other stations. One new subway line, the Namboku line, has installed transparent safety barriers at each of their stations which open automatically when the train comes to a stop.

Railway officials rack their brains to think of ways to pack more people into the coaches. Some cars of the heavily-used Yamanote loop line have hinged seats so that they can be raised out of the way and the car crammed with even more bodies. "It's 10 a.m. Can passengers in the standing car please take a seat," goes the announcement that unofficially marks the end of the morning rush hour. The railroads cut more doors on the sides of the cars so that people can enter and exit more quickly. The trains on the Hibiya subway line have five doors on either side, rather than three. That way, it is said, passengers can get on and off about ten seconds faster. The railway managers consider this a considerable achievement since it allows more trains to pass by a specific station during the most heavily used times; however, this only increases the misery of people wanting to cross the tracks. Because of the incessant flow of trains, the crossing gates are perpetually down during the busiest commuting hours. Frustrated pedestrians or people on bicycles sometimes risk their lives by going around the barricades and darting across the tracks in the brief interludes between trains.

For years, the transportation ministry has urged companies to stagger their working hours or adopt flex-time schedules in order to ease the load during the busiest hours. The ministry claims that if only 15 percent to 20 percent of the people working in central Tokyo started at an unconventional hour, train crowding would fall to a comparatively relaxed 150 percent of capacity. These pleas usually fall on deaf ears, or if companies do adopt flex-time, the salarymen tend to come to work at the regular hour anyway. Of late, the ministry and the railroads have been getting more serious. JR East set an example by having its own employees start work 20 minutes later than usual. A Council for the Promotion of Off-Peak Commuting was also set up and sponsors such events as the "Off-Peak Commuting Promotion Month." The East Japan Railway plans to add cars that are 20 cm wider. But it is not to make the journey more comfortable for passengers. The company thinks it can jam 10 more passengers inside each car.

Conventional bird's eye maps of Tokyo are virtually useless for getting around. That's why millions of diagrammatic maps are printed showing the 1,180 rail and subway stations that are located throughout the capital region and the dozens of rail lines, each with their own shade of color. The older lines are in primary reds, blues, and yellows. The newer ones shade off into pastels, mauves and yellowish green. They look like the electrical wiring plans for a supercomputer, and they are about as easy for a foreigner to decipher, since they are usually printed exclusively in

Japanese characters. The Yamanote line is invariably shown as a perfect circle with the Chuo line, leading to the western suburbs, cutting it in half like some kind of yin-yang ideogram. It is not a literal representation of the city, but, like the conventional picture of an atom, it conveys a kind of cosmic truth that more literal charts fail to do.

The first railway line built specifically to serve commuters was the Chuo (central) line that stretches from Tokyo Station across the Musashi plain toward the western suburbs. It was constructed by private interests in the 1880s to connect Tokyo with Yamanashi prefecture. It had stops in Kokubunji, Tachikawa and Hachioji, then distant towns. The Great Kanto Earthquake hastened the movement of people out of the burned-out low city toward the west along this and other rail corridors. That, in turn, required more rail lines for more commuters. The most heavily used is the Yamanote loop line. It also traces its beginnings to the late 19th century, when it was originally planned to link Shinagawa with Maebashi in Gunma prefecture. It became a full loop in 1925 with the construction of the elevated section between Ueno and Kanda. In many ways the Yamanote loop defines the parameters of Tokyo better than any political boundary. Anything inside this great circle route is by common agreement the inner city. Anything outside of it, the beginning of the suburbs or, on the east side, the fading old city. Hardly anyone moving around town can avoid a ride on the Yamanote line cars, which are instantly recognizable by the green stripe on the outside. Knowing this rail line is a matter of fundamental literacy about Tokyo. Almost all of the main centers of the city are on it: Shinjuku, Ueno, Shibuya, Ikebukuro and Tokyo Stations, to name a few. It takes about an hour to circle the 34.5 km around it, and it is probable that the true Tokyoite can recite all 29 stations along the way from memory.

The Chuo and Yamanote lines are operated by privatized branches of the former national Japan Railways (JR) Corp., but most of the newer ones laid out since the end of the war have been built by private railway companies. Usually, they are also the owners of large department stores. It makes for a formidable combination. The rail company erects a large store at a station terminus then extends a line out to the suburbs, which draws in the customers. At many locations, it is nearly impossible to exit from the station without passing through one of these establishments. This sure fire combination has turned many an unimportant neighborhood into a miniature metropolis. The best example is Ikebukuro. It wasn't even a gateway to the provinces like Shinjuku or Shinagawa when, by a stroke of good fortune, a station on the Yamanote line was opened there. Then the Seibu interests erected a department store in front of the station.

Today, Ikebukuro is like two kingdoms divided by a rail road. On one side behold the Realm of Tobu, dominated by the huge flank of the Tobu Department Store, the world's largest. The Tobu Tojo rail line emanates from the basement of the store, heading toward Kawagoe and the suburbs of Saitama prefecture. On the opposite side of the tracks is the Empire of Seibu. The large mass of the Seibu Department Store looms over the station square like the Kremlin Wall dominates Red Square. The Saikyo rail line departs from its own Seibu-Ikebukuro station under the buildings. Similarly, much of the western part of Tokyo is under the thrall of Tokyu. Three of its rail lines fan out from its commercial nexus in Shibuya toward Yokohama and suburbs to the west. In this way the great city has grown and spread.

A lucky few commuters avoid the cattle cars and ride to work in comfort from the far exurbs on the shinkansen, or bullet train. Not for them two hours of torture standing up cheek-by-jowl with

200 other passengers. On the bullet train everyone has his own well-padded seat with arm rests. Probably he has been ferried to the outlying station by his wife, driving the family Mazda, looking to the world like a country squire riding into New York from Connecticut. Shinkansen commuting has made it possible for some people to live as far away as 180 km from Tokyo station and still travel to and from work in less than two hours. People can live in the smaller cities, like Utsunomiya, where the pace of life is slower and where a spacious house is still something that the average family can afford. But monthly passes can cost as much as $1,000. Some companies underwrite this expense. The Ministry of Labor estimated in 1992 that 600 firms paid the full cost of commuting by bullet train and another 1,200 offered at least partial compensation. As the trains get sleeker and faster, the commuting possibilities extend farther and farther. The fastest train, the Nozomi, reaches speeds of up to 270 km/hr. It can cover the distance between Tokyo and Osaka in about 2 and a half hours. Towns as distant as 300 km north of the capital thus are coming within commuting range. Even faster models on the drawing boards might literally float along the rails at 500 km/hr. When they come into operation, Osaka will be only about one hour away — no farther in commuting terms than any of Tokyo's near suburbs today. The only drawback will be the cost.

Despite its obvious attractions, however, shinkansen commuting draws only a tiny fraction of the millions who ride the rails to and from work each day. Many who ride them already have roots in the small communities along the commuter route. Not very many people have actually moved to the exurbs to take advantage of the comparatively gracious living there, and some of the housing developments built to attract them have gone bankrupt. A two-hour commute is still a two-hour commute, even if one can do it sitting down.

In the suburbs, the train culture subtly begins to blend with a newer automobile culture. Many of the rice paddies have been sold and subdivided into housing developments with modern, suburban-style homes built on the land. The traditional commercial centers built around railroad stations are beginning to find competition from something akin to American-style shopping malls. Here on Sunday, the family piles into the Toyota compact to go shopping at the local "Home Center" discount store with its relatively spacious parking lot, or they go out to eat at the "Royal Host" family restaurant, all sitting together in a molded plastic booth. A few new housing developments seem to have been copied directly from America or Australia, with large, two-story houses, neat lawns, backyard swimming pools and two-car garages (although sometimes the cars are literally stacked one on top of the other). They are popular with doctors and with executives who developed a taste of more gracious and spacious living from tours abroad and have the means to afford them.

Most people still use the commuter trains to go to work in Tokyo, but about 2 million brave the *shuto,* or metropolitan expressway. The first segment was completed in 1962, a couple of years before the Olympic Games. Today, approximately 220 km of roads weave their way through the metropolis. It is something of a marvel that any kind of highway system could be built at all given Tokyo's peculiar circular layout, its enormous congestion and the archaic property laws. Most of them are four-lane affairs, supported on pylons above ordinary ground-level streets. But many wind their way along or over rivers or canals where it was not necessary to obtain rights-of-way from private property owners. One highway runs along the Nihonbashi River, providing an ugly dark canopy directly over the famous Nihonbashi Bridge.

Congestion is endemic on all roads, as anyone knows who has taken the airport bus into the city from Narita airport. Along Route 4, which runs from Shinjuku through the core of the downtown, the average speed often drops to less than 10 km per hour. The Metropolitan Expressway Public Corp. counts 15,000 traffic jams in a year or one about every 30 minutes. Frustrated drivers read books or listen to tapes to while away the hours idling in traffic. People have been known to abandon taxis in mid-ride and head for the nearest railway station. The expressway corporation is frantically building two new loop roads around the capital. But progress is frustrated by land prices. Property rights and a desire not to blot out rivers produce some strange contortions, such as the Katsushika "Harp" Bridge, one of the few bridges in the world constructed in an "S" curve. Many newer stretches will probably be sunk under ground.

About 50,000 taxis ply the streets of Tokyo, half of them company-operated, the other half driven by owners. In the years after the war, Tokyo cabbies had a kind of devil-may-care reputation. People called them "kamikazes" after the famous suicide pilots, and riding in one sometimes seemed a little like taking one's life in one's hand. Now many of them have passed into advanced middle age, and rides have become a lot less adventurous, especially for foreigners confronted with uncomprehending drivers who sometimes seem ignorant of your destination, even if written down in Japanese characters by a helpful hotel concierge. Taxi cabs had become one of the stuffiest, most conservative and consumer-resistant industries in the country. And with a standard, fixed $6 or 660 yen flagfall, it could also be pretty expensive. In fact, taxi driving was fast becoming a dying industry. Statistics show that ridership, which peaked in the boom year 1989, is falling off dramatically.

The end of the century brought glimmerings of change. For the first time in years new companies were allowed to compete in the city's inner wards. In 1998 a queer-looking hatchback converted from a recreational vehicle began appearing in the taxi lines, calling itself the "One-Coin Taxis." It offered Tokyo's lowest flagfall, 580 yen for the first two km, and, despite its odd shape, plenty of leg room for passengers in the back. Then came the "340 yen" taxi, so named for the fare charged to take a rider one kilometer. The fare for two km still worked out to the standard 660 yen, but at least it offered the passenger the option of a shorter, cheaper ride. For those preferring luxury, MK Taxi of Kyoto offers a chauffeur-like service, each driver dressed up like a hotel bell captain.

It often seems that Tokyo is nothing more than an extraordinarily efficient machine for moving people from one place to another. Everyday thousands of trains transport millions of people, all keeping within seconds of their official schedules. But there isn't room for error. The trains must arrive at evenly spaced intervals, scoop up their human cargoes and move on to the next stop. If a delay occurs for any reason, a fast-moving ripple effect occurs. Trains back up, yet the station platforms continue to fill with people, becoming unbearably overcrowded. Broken bones are not unknown. The average Tokyoite may look stoic waiting impassively on the platform for the train to arrive, but he is at heart a restless individual. He begins to get agitated if he has to wait more than ten minutes for the next train. (Other waits that set the teeth on edge, according to the Hokuhodo Institute of Life and Living are eleven minutes for a bus, thirteen for a taxi, four for a public telephone and five minutes in a supermarket checkout line.)

Certainly, chaos can ensue if the system is disrupted for any reason. Railway worker strikes are less common than they were in the years just after the war, but when they do occur, they wreck havoc. One strike in 1992 disrupted the routines of more than six million people. In 1974, some irate passengers lost their well-known cool during a go-slow action by the public railway unions and went on a rampage, smashing offices in Tokyo Station and others.

Drivers spend hundreds of hours in training. They master the rules of the road, memorize a 200-page railway manual, and, above all, inculcate an almost spiritual feeling for punctuality. They may be the closest thing to human robots in existence, and proud of it. In the prize-winning novel, **The Motorman** by Tomomi Fujiwara, a driver has nightmares about being late. "His glass eye bounced out and rolled along the platform like a marble, just out of reach. He lurched after it, but suddenly stopped and glanced at his watch. Just 30 seconds to departure. In a split-second he decided there was no time to retrieve his eye and scurried back to his compartment . . . . As he pulled the train out of the station, a terrible thought struck him. Isn't driving one-eyed a violation of the rules?"

Mechanical breakdowns and driver errors are relatively rare; it is usually passengers who delay the trains. Attendants keep a lookout for drunks and others who might accidentally fall off the platform. But one thing is usually out of their control: the "jumper," a person who kills himself by leaping in front of an on-coming train or who lays down on the tracks. About one person a day kills himself in this manner in the capital. Passengers are only aware of the delay through a terse announcement: "We regret to inform you that the train has been delayed by a human accident." Newspapers run headlines that read something like this: "Man commits suicide on the Chuo line; 50,000 commuters delayed during rush hour." Train authorities are unsentimental about the delays that these suicides can cause. Relatives are sometimes presented with a bill for the cleanup and the disruption that the inconvenient death caused. Although they are not legally bound to do so, many feel a moral obligation to pay. The Chuo line is reputed to be the favorite of jumpers because it charges less.

Nothing illustrates the collective discipline of the Japanese people better than their capacity to endure this torture day after day. The only reason the system functions at all is because people are willing to submerge themselves into the collectivity. One can see this on the subway escalator, where people line up with military precision on the right-hand-side of the moving stairs. Once a nine-year-old American, exhibiting the unbridled exuberance of his race, released a garter snake in a crowded train car on the Chuo line and yelled, "Snake! Snake!" He might as well have yelled "Fire!" in a crowded theater. The entire train had to be diverted to a yard as workmen searched high and low for the slithering critter. The Japan Times was not amused. It seems that the whole thing was a deliberate prank such as may be common in American cities and others. However, the humor was lost on most adults here, whether witnesses or not," the newspaper opined soberly. There cannot be much toleration for individuals who, for whatever reason, impede the flow.

Women are often forced to exhibit a special stoicism while riding on crowded commuter trains. The sheer anonymity inside the typical commuter car provides a perfect setting for gropers. Of all the forms of sexual harassment that Tokyo women must endure, fondling on the trains is probably the most common. It is not unusual for a woman to feel a stranger rubbing up against her body or thrusting a hand under her skirt. An unusual best seller in 1994 was **A Groper's Diary** by Samu Yamamoto. The mousy-looking man recounted in intimate detail and apparently without any sense of shame how he molested women on trains every day for 26 years. He counted on his victims being too embarrassed to cry out or too worried about naming the wrong person. Yamamoto said he wouldn't dream of trying the same thing on an American train because the women who ride them are too tough. "But Japanese women tolerate us — or I'd be in jail now." Some women's groups have pressed the railway companies to create special women-only cars for their own protection. Determined to curtail such incidents, the Keio line introduced women-only cars on a trial basis in late 2000. The carriages were available at night, when men, emboldened by drink at after-work parties, might be more inclined to grope. It is an old story, really. Groping by Tokyo University boys caused railway authorities to introduce women-only cars during the morning and evening rush hours in the late Meiji period.

All of this stoicism exacts a toll. There is, for example, a correlation between lengthy hours on the commuter lines and excessive drinking and smoking. In order to avoid the crowded rush hour going home, some men kill time after work by staying in town for a drink with colleagues. Or, sometimes they break up the long trip home by stopping at a station along the way for a drink or a cigarette. Tsukuba University studied 5,500 men residing in Narashino, a bedroom community in Chiba prefecture in 1994 and demonstrated what they said was a clear link between smoking and drinking and long commuting hours. Most of those respondents who said they drank more than six medium bottles of beer or its equivalent in whiskey or sake per week spent more than 90 minutes riding home from the office. Those with long commutes also tended to get less sleep at night or skipped breakfast in the morning in order to get to the station to catch an early train.

Consider this poignant plea from a salaryman's wife published in the *Asahi Shimbun*, Japan's major newspaper: "My husband works fourteen hours a day. In addition, he puts in 100 hours of unpaid overtime a month. He spends three hours a day commuting. Each day he struggles to fight off drowsiness. He is bone tired. He sleeps like a baby on Saturday and Sundays. He devotes his physical and spiritual energies solely to his bank. He comes home only to recharge his physical strength . . . When our youngest daughter was hospitalized, my husband had to take a half-day off. What did his supervisor say? 'Did you have to take a half-day for such a thing?' He is skinny no matter how much he eats. The gap between breakfast and dinner can extend up to seventeen hours . . . Sudden death in middle age is one of the hot topics in Japan now. I fear such a death could become a reality for my husband. There seems to be nothing I can do but watch this happen."

Tokyo's people take enormous pride in the belief that theirs is one of the safest cities in the world. City fathers constantly trot out the statistics: burglaries 200 times fewer than New York, murder at least 25 times less frequent, for example. There are many stresses involved in living in the world's largest city, not excluding the constant threat of being crushed in a giant earthquake. But getting mugged on the commuter train isn't one of them. Or is it? In late 1994, one Takejiro Okazaki was about to insert his pass into the automatic turnstyle at Aomono-Yokocho Station when a shot rang out. The 47-year-old urologist slumped to the floor and died a short while later in a nearby hospital. His assailant was a former patient who bore a grudge against the doctor regarding a hernia operation. An isolated incident, perhaps, but also a portent. Stories about shootings and guns began appearing more frequently in the newspapers and on television.

Then one Monday morning in early 1995, Kazumasa Takahashi, an assistant station-master on the Chiyoda underground line in central Tokyo was on duty when the 8:10 train pulled in. Many of the passengers were civil servants whose offices are in the government ministries in the nearby Kasumigaseki district next to the Imperial Palace. Before the doors slammed shut, Takahashi noticed that some liquid had spilled onto the train floor. He mopped it up and waved the train on. Shortly after, he collapsed on the platform and died. Within minutes, thousands of commuters were staggering out of the subway exits, gasping for breath, coughing, rubbing their eyes or foaming at the mouth. Urban terrorists had planted sarin nerve gas at five widely scattered locations along three downtown subway lines in what must surely have been the world's first use of a weapon of mass destruction delivered in a lunch box.

It would be a long time before any Tokyo commuter entered a subway car again without feeling at least a small pang of trepidation. The authorities didn't help by constantly reminding the riders to be on the lookout for suspicious behavior and strange packages in the overhead racks. For a while, transit authorities removed all of the rubbish bins from Tokyo's subways, fearing that they might be convenient hiding places for terrorist bombs. That forced passengers to stuff their pockets full of used tissues, gum wrappers and empty juice boxes until they could dispose of them at the office. Ironically, station masters claimed that the stations became even cleaner without the trash bins. Most people had little choice but to get back on the trains for the ride into work, though there was a noticeable shift to above-ground lines, presumably less vulnerable to a gas attack. But it must have seemed to many that something indefinable about the quality of life in Tokyo had snapped. Urban terrorism was no longer the stuff of thrillers and news reports from foreign lands but a part of their everyday life. The hell of commuting had suddenly come to seem a good deal more like hell.

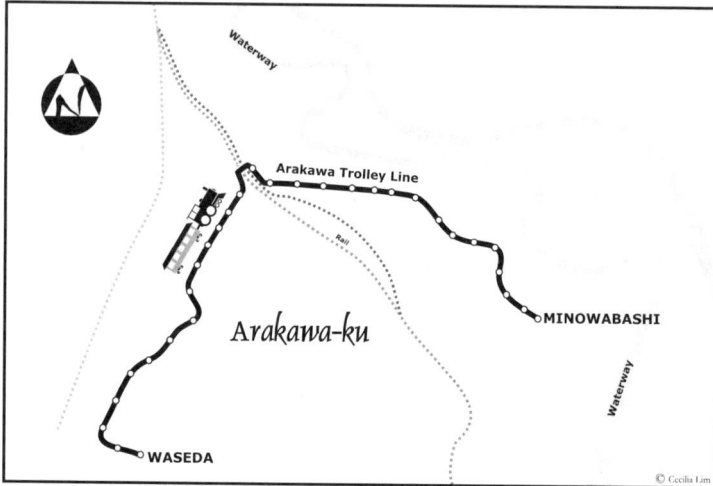

## The Ding Dong Trolley

The Arakawa line is all that remains of the once extensive network of trolley car lines that criss-crossed Tokyo. At one time close to 40 lines served the commuting public, but as new subway lines were built and buses began to take over, the trolley lines were consolidated and shut down one-by-one until only the Arakawa line was left in 1972.

First opened in 1911, the Arakawa line, nicknamed the *Chin Chin Densha*, or 'Ding Dong Trolley' for its clanging bell, runs from Waseda to Minowa-bashi crossing Arakawa Ward, a northeastern district of the city bordering on the Sumida River. The route includes none of the major shopping or sightseeing districts of Tokyo. In fact, among its stops are the sites of some of the city's least appealing past and present attractions: the Tokugawa shoguns' execution grounds, temples reserved for funerals for Yoshiwara prostitutes, and, today, Tokyo's major crematoria. Older Tokyo residents still associate Arakawa with the "unclean" professions handled by the outcasts who lived in the area: disposing of corpses, working with leather and rag-picking.

Still, the trolley route is gaining popularity as a nostalgic day trip for modern Tokyoites trying to experience something of the past. The line has developed a cult following complete with souvenirs including bean-paste cakes in the shape of the trolley car, beer, sake and tea with the Ding Dong Trolley label, and the usual assortment of badges and model cars. There are even a few Web sites devoted to the line. When I made the trip on a Sunday, among the regular riders were a few families and couples with guidebooks in hand riding just for the fun of it.

The Arakawa line, however, is by no means just a relic or mere tourist attraction. About 67,000 people ride it daily even though it seems to go from nowhere to nowhere. I got on at the western end near Waseda University, one of Japan's oldest and most prestigious private universities. While some parts of Waseda have an old-city feel this particular section is all wide boulevards and new condos. The character of the neighborhoods begins to shift just before Koshintsuka Station, about 15 minutes into the ride, when the trolley tracks turn off the main street, and the car makes its way through narrow residential lanes. On the platform at Koshintsuka, a small restaurant offers an old Tokyo winter specialty: *miso oden*, a stew of vegetables left simmering all day in a miso-flavored broth. The aroma as much as anything says "Shitamachi," as the old city is sometimes defined.

After Koshintsuka, the backs of small houses close in on both sides of the track. The width of the rail is only 372mm, the same as that of an English horse carriage circa 1911 when the track was first laid. The narrow car blends well with the old-city narrow streets: cross streets reveal shrines, peaceful residential districts and busy shopping streets. It may be my imagination, but it also seems that there are more women wearing a kimono here than in other parts of the city.

Each of the 29 stops along the way has something to offer, and with a one-day pass a rider can get off and on all day. The Kajiwara stop, close to the Sumida River and a Kirin Beer brewery, is the place to buy bean cakes that come in a box shaped like the trolley. Arakawa Yuenchi-mae is the closest stop to the Arakawa Amusement Park, a no-frills pre-theme park amusement park, opened in 1922, with a Ferris wheel, a merry-go-round, spinning tea cups, a petting zoo and even a miniature Ding Dong Trolley. It advertises itself as cheap, safe, Old Tokyo fun.

Forty-eight minutes from Waseda, the trolley comes to the end of the line at Minowa-bashi, a lively neighborhood with a shopping arcade optimistically labeling the area in English as "Joyful Minowa." I wandered around for a while, marveling at the low prices in the fruit and vegetable stores, one of the benefits the residents get for living in a remote, decidedly down-scale section of Tokyo. Before jumping on the subway for the ride back to my side of town, I succumbed to the lure of the *obanyaki* stand. For only 80 yen, I bought this traditional Tokyo snack, a bean paste-filled round pancake-like treat, from a man who looked like he might have been selling obanyaki on the day the Arakawa line opened in 1911. But even he had acknowledged the changing tastes of the tourists from the western part of the city. In addition to the traditional bean paste filling, you can now get custard, chocolate or even — unthinkable only a few years ago — cheese-filled obanyaki.

— S.F.M.

# 3

# Money

From the East Garden of the Imperial Palace in what used to be the Shogun's castle, it was possible, more than 100 years ago, to see the waters of Tokyo Bay. From the same vantage point today a different and wholly incomprehensible vista presents itself to the visitor from old Edo, as Tokyo was called from the 15th to the 19th centuries. The Imperial Palace now stands eight kilometers from open water. In between is a phalanx of buildings marching off in the distance. Between the palace grounds and the waters of the bay stands the Marunouchi financial district and beyond that the glittery Ginza shopping quarter and beyond that more tracts of commercial buildings and then, finally, the bay. During the day, this district is teeming with people. In the morning they stream out of the red-brick west entrance of Tokyo Station and a hundred other subway exits in a steady procession, faces set, neckties straight, briefcases in hand, ready for another day of service. They make their way briskly and purposefully down the streets and disappear into the office buildings. By nightfall, the dark-suited legions swarm out of the buildings and stores, some perhaps pausing at the bars and clubs in Ginza close by, before heading back to the suburbs. After midnight, the population will have shrunk to a few thousand, mostly janitors and night watchmen.

In some ways, it is a singularly unimpressive neighborhood to be the center of the world's largest city and the hub of one of the most impressive wealth-creating machines that the world has ever known. No tall, aluminum-coated towers rise here, rather a succession of squat, non-descript cubes without adornment. Almost none of the buildings is more than a dozen stories tall. They do, however, give off a feeling of something solid that matches the demeanor of the people who work here. Tokyo may trail New York and Los Angeles for cultural influence. Washington may still exert political power and dispatch armies here and there. But Tokyo is the capital of capital. Here is where the country's trade surpluses are stored, managed and manipulated. Here is where huge corporations plot their world-wide strategies, where they raise their capital, where business intelligence is collected, gleaned and analyzed. This is where the brightest of its youth head to realize their ambitions. This is also where deals are concluded and where, sometimes, discreet bribes are made at expensive but unobtrusive restaurants.

The word Marunouchi means "inside the walls" in Japanese. During Edo times, the most powerful and loyal noblemen built their spacious estates there inside the grounds of the Shogun's castle, whose fortifications in those days extended far beyond the boundaries of the present Imperial Palace grounds. After the Meiji Restoration in 1868, these estates fell into disrepair as the *daimyo*, or feudal barons, were freed to return to their provincial domains, and the new Imperial Army took it over for barracks and a parade field. In time, though, the army moved to other quarters, and what is now arguably the world's most valuable tract of real estate was turned into a scruffy wasteland. Pictures of what was then called the "Marunouchi Meadows" a hundred years ago show weeds where now some of the world's largest corporations have their headquarters.

In 1890, Yanosuke Iwasaki, the brother of the founder of the Mitsubishi empire, bought 86 acres of land there and in surrounding neighborhoods for the equivalent of about $8,000. Then the purchase was considered an extravagance. Today, however, that would buy only a few square centimeters of land in the same neighborhood. In 1894, Mitsubishi built its headquarters in a redbrick European-style building that was to help give the district, for a while, the nickname of "Tokyo Londontown." Only the redbrick west entrance to Tokyo Station, completed in 1914, gives any impression of what the original Marunouchi district must have looked like. But the district is still very much a Mitsubishi village. Mitsubishi Estate Co. still owns 24 buildings there and eight more in nearby Otemachi, providing space for 4,100 companies. The company carries these properties and others in Japan and abroad on its books at a nominal value of about $4 billion. This figure is surely understated, although it is difficult to gauge the value of land in this area with precision because it very rarely changes hands. The National Land Agency once estimated the value a square meter of land in the san-chome section of Marunouchi at ¥38.6 million , or about $290,000 (nearly $35,000 per square foot). Surely, there hasn't been such a lucrative real estate deal since the Dutch bought Manhattan Island from the Native Americans for the equivalent of $24 in knives, clothes and beads.

Anyone happening to pass through the district on the second Friday of the month might notice an unusual number of sober-looking but expensive cars parked on the side streets. Many of them are black Nissan Presidents, the Japanese executive's limousine of choice. White-lace coverlets are draped over the empty backseats. Chauffeurs loll about gossiping with one another or eating lunch from wooden bento-boxes. In an elegant restaurant at the top floor of the Mitsubishi Building, some forty or so top executives gather for their monthly luncheon. They are the presidents and chairmen of the 49 companies that make up the Mitsubishi Group, the largest *keiretsu*, or conglomerate, in the country. These captains of industry are coming together for their *Kinyokai*, their private executive club. The meeting will be presided over by the chairman of the Mitsubishi Corp., the trading company that is, symbolically at least, the leader of the group. The beverage served will undoubtedly be Kirin beer. The brewery is a prominent member of the Mitsubishi group.

This is not, the company's publicists take pains to point out, a meeting of the board of directors. Every person attending the meeting answers to his own board because he represents a company that is completely independent. They are related to the other members of the group only by a web of social connections, a common name and logo (the famous three diamonds, the *mitsu bishi*, means 'three diamonds' in Japanese), and a certain amount of common stock holdings, usually no more than a few percentage points. It wasn't always so. Before World War II, Mitsubishi was one of the largest of the pre-war *zaibatsu*, a fully integrated, family-owned holding company with interests in banking, shipping, insurance and trade. The American occupation forces broke up the company, as they did the other zaibatsu, and stripped the Iwasaki family of its control. Today, nearly two dozen companies bear the Mitsubishi name, held together by a common tradition and a web of crossholdings. A total of 29 are considered part of the group's core, and 49 are members of the Kinyokai. Hundreds more are loosely affiliated as suppliers to one or more of the group companies. When one of the members, Mitsubishi Metal, actually bought and merged with another, Mitsubishi Mining Co., it set off alarm bells of a revival of the zaibatsu system. The core companies and their affiliates gross about $250 billion. If Mitsubishi were an independent country, it would rank approximately 15th in terms of gross national product, just behind India but ahead of Sweden.

What really goes on at the Kinyokai meeting is a closely guarded secret. No outsiders are allowed to attend, and the minutes are kept in strict confidence. Participants always say that the meetings, which usually last about an hour and a half, are purely social. Some gossip, some talk about politics, perhaps a lecture and all enjoy a very good lunch. In 1989, the chairman of Mitsubishi Corp., Yohei Mimura, claimed to have walked out of one such meeting blissfully ignorant of one of the group's biggest impending moves. Only when it was announced publicly, did he learn that Mitsubishi Estate was buying a controlling interest in Rockefeller Center in New York for about $850 million. Yotaro Iida, chairman of Mitsubishi Heavy Industries, once described a meeting of the Kinyokai in these terms: "It's like when a family, relatives of a whole clan, get together at funerals or weddings and check that everybody's doing all right, nobody's in trouble with the police and so on." Perhaps so, but certainly foreigners look with some suspicion on the workings of the group and other executive clubs as, indeed, they do with the entire keiretsu system. Some light on the inner workings was shed in a 1976 book, **The History of the Kinyokai** by Chujiro Fujino, who was club secretary at the time. He wrote that they served three main functions. They determine group strategy such as whether the companies should move into promising new fields of business, perhaps biotechnology. In 1985, the entire Kinyokai membership formed a cooperative called Space Communications, and a few years later it launched its first satellite. Second, they deal with political problems arising from government regulations and policy. And, third, they pass judgement on the mergers of member companies and adjudicate disputes over who should succeed as chairman or president. All of the big six keiretsu have their own executive clubs. The other five are Mitsui and Sumitomo, both inheritors of proud, prewar names, and newcomers Fuyo, Sanwa and Dai Ichi Kangin.

At least, the participants do not have to travel very far to get back to their offices after the luncheon is over. Many of the group's members are clustered together in Mitsubishi's Marunouchi village. Here is the headquarters of Mitsubishi Heavy Industries, there are Mitsubishi Petro-Chemicals and Mitsubishi Paper Mills. Another building houses Nikon Corp., makers of the famous camera. It, too, belongs to the Mitsubishi stable. Towering over everyone is Bank of Tokyo-Mitsubishi Bank, whose gleaming new headquarters is twice as tall as most other buildings in the district and sticks out conspicuously. The buildings here are almost always fully let, and there is usually a long waiting list of companies that would like to boast the priceless cachet of a Marunouchi address. Yet, their owners consider the properties to be vastly underutilized. They chafe at the regulations that limit the heights of the buildings to a dozen or so stories. For it is not, as is often said, a reluctance to tower over and thus allow mere mortals to peer down into the sacred grounds of the Imperial Palace next door that keeps them from building higher. And in any case, if one were so inclined, he or she could look down into the palace grounds from the observation platform of the nearby Kasumigaseki Building, which was Japan's first, and for many years, its only skyscraper. No, what keeps Marunouchi from looking like mid-town Manhattan is a mundane thing known as a floor-area-ratio, or FAR. These are calculated according to a complex formula that establishes floor space as a ratio of the underlying ground. The FAR rule in this part of Tokyo is 1,000 percent, which means that the usable floor space can be ten times the square footage of the ground the building stands on. In 1988, the Mitsubishi Estate Co. and its allied property owners in the Marunouchi, Otemachi and Yurakucho districts presented a plan to replace the existing collection of squat, low-lying buildings with about 60 new skyscrapers of 50 to 60 stories each. The development would, according to the company's brochure, allow Marunouchi to "exert its full role as a center of the international city of Tokyo," not to mention compete with other rising centers, such as the West Shinjuku district.

The difficulty was that this ambitious plan would have required a doubling of the floor area ratios in the district to 2,000 percent, a tall order. The 1,000 percent limit hasn't been changed in Tokyo for 25 years. In most areas of the city the FARs are around 300 to 400 percent, and even in the cluster of skyscrapers in West Shinjuku, the ratio is, by special dispensation, only 1,100 percent. The local Chiyoda Ward authorities supported the proposal, in part because they saw the added office space as taking some pressure off residential areas and stemming the outflow of permanent residents. The Tokyo Metropolitan Government, which had its own vision of Tokyo as an international city built around separate urban hubs, including a massive new one on Tokyo Bay, has been unenthusiastic about the project so far, and one can't help but wonder what kind of strain a doubling of office space in this part of the city would put on the commuter system. Tokyo Station is already one of the biggest hubs for commuters in the city's center. When Mitsubishi revealed its artist's concept, it set off a wave of protest. *The Japan Times* said it showed "A Tokyo Without A Heart." The story beneath the headline read, "There, rising in front of the verdant Imperial Palace grounds, which somehow escaped the treatment, [would stand] a bank of skyscrapers several rows deep. It appeared like some scene out of a graveyard, and that precisely is the correct symbolism . . . . Tokyo is not the most beautiful city in the world, but it does have its own attributes. We decry its high costs, but destroying the city to solve that or any other problem doesn't really make sense."

A few kilometers away, in the Nihonbashi district, is Tokyo's original financial center and the cradle of Japanese capitalism. The Bank of Japan, the nation's central bank, is still located there, close to the Nihonbashi River, and is housed in an imposing stone building designed in the neo-classical mode of the 1890s. It sits appropriately on what was once Japan's first gold mint. The Nihonbashi district is the turf of Mitsui, the old rival to the Mitsubishi business interests. The flagship store of the Mitsukoshi department store chain is located here. Nihonbashi Bridge, where traditionally all distances from Edo to the rest of Japan were measured, is a very undistinguished-looking structure. Built in 1911, it has for many years been obscured by an ugly expressway overpass constructed at the time of the 1964 Olympic Games.

Next to it stands the equally unprepossessing headquarters of Nomura Securities Co. Outside the dull, dark-red brick building, one could often spot a television crew looking bored. They came alert whenever one of the senior officers of Nomura entered a limousine to be driven to testify before one or another committee of the Diet about one money scandal or another. Still, Nomura is, unquestionably, one of the biggest and richest stock brokerage houses in the world, larger than Merrill Lynch and many others in the West. Nomura was, for a while, the most profitable company in Japan, surpassing even Toyota Motor Co. Somehow, it seemed fitting that at the height of the orgy of speculation in the Bubble Era, a company that traded in paper would surpass companies that made mere things. But then, Toyota itself earned a third of its profits that year from what its accountants called "revenue outside of sales," in other words, by playing the stock market rather than by making cars.

The stock exchange itself is located in a modern-looking, triangular-shaped building in the middle of narrow streets and alleyways in a rather drab corner of the Nihonbashi district. The Japanese call this particular area the Kabutocho, and it is often described as Tokyo's Wall Street, though it lacks something of New York's panache. During the Meiji period, Mitsui Co., the giant zaibatsu, saw the potential of this area near the old Nihonbashi bridge market and erected a much-admired headquarters building there in 1872. The building passed into the hands of a famous early capitalist named Eiichi Shibusawa, and it was he who in 1878 helped open the city's first stock exchange there. Banks, insurance companies and other business enterprises also opened, but the Kabutocho never really developed into a hub. In 1890, Mitsubishi made a prescient purchase of the meadowlands near the palace and was able to offer Japan's rising capitalists better accommodations. One by one they gravitated there. The Mitsui building was destroyed in 1923, in the Great Kanto Earthquake. Only the stock exchange itself remains of the larger financial institutions along with a warren of smaller brokerage houses. Little else is worth a second glance.

On the first floor of the exchange is a small museum tracing the history of Japan's capital markets. Ancient capitalists wearing dress kimonos appear in old photographs with determined looks on their faces. Other photographs show the buildings that once stood on this site before earthquakes brought them down. Perhaps the most poignant exhibit is a blown-up reproduction of the American Occupation announcement of the re-opening of the Tokyo exchange after it had been closed for nearly four years after the war. It is a plain, typewritten letter dated May 12, 1949, and it reads in part: "It is emphasized that the Japanese public will have the safeguards of a modern exchange law, which will provide adequate protection against malpractice and hazards in the pre-war exchanges. The opening of the security exchanges is expected to contribute to the orderly flow of capital into productive channels under a comprehensive system of safeguards to eliminate the unscrupulous and haphazard practices jeopardizing the interests of the general public." The Diet later dutifully adopted almost verbatim the provisions of the U.S. Securities & Exchange Law, but soon after regaining its independence in 1951, Japan gutted many of them. Today the letter seems poignant in light of the kickbacks, favoritism and other scandals that were to engulf the securities industry when the stock market bubble finally burst.

The ivory-colored vertical bars and mirrors on the face of the Mullion Building glisten in the gauzy light of late afternoon. Shoppers scurry across the Sukiyabashi intersection and into the building's wide portals. The site was once the location of a Tokyo landmark, the Nichigeki Theater. With five cinemas on an upper floor, the Mullion carries on the tradition, even if the famous chorus line is long gone. Two department stores now occupy the two inter-linked hemispheres, the larger one being fourteen stories tall. Both stores are relative latecomers to the Ginza. Their move into the Mullion in 1984 was the first expansion in the city's most prestigious shopping district in many years. It added some welcome glamour to a part of Tokyo whose image was in need of a little burnishing. Young people, who had been deserting the Ginza for the trendier shopping areas like Shibuya, began to return.

Every morning the doors open with a flourish as uniformed female greeters welcome the shoppers to the delights within. A bank of video screens near the entrance guides customers to all of the 122 departments, starting with the basement food mart and extending upwards to Sotheby's outlet on the seventh floor, where a customer can bid on London auctions via a satellite link. The basement stalls offer every kind of food from tempura to Aunt Stella's cookies. Perfectly round grapes, each one the size of a walnut and of the deepest purple glisten in their baskets. Lovely oval mangoes, $5 a pair, are each safely nestled in styrofoam cradles. Upstairs there are concession areas for Louis Fernard suits, Turnbull & Sasser shirts, Ralph Laurent and Issey Miyake dresses, fine European porcelain and jewelry from Garrard, "Jewelers to the Queen", each displayed in its own individual shops.

Only a few blocks separate the capital of capital from the capital of consumption, from where money is made to where it is spent, sometimes quite lavishly. Consumption has been one of the defining aspects of Tokyo since Edo times, when half of the city's population belonged to the warrior class: feudal lords, their samurai retainers and servants. They produced nothing. Everyone else, aside from the temple priests, existed mainly to sell them things or otherwise cater to their needs and desires. Many of the larger stores trace their ancestry back 300 years. The mighty Mitsukoshi started as the Echigoya Fabric Shop, entering Edo from the provinces in the 17th century. Customers used to enter a kind of vestibule while the clerks, sitting on a raised *tatami* platform, brought out merchandise for the customer to inspect at the platform's edge. Mitsukoshi, founded in 1904 under its present name, was the first to put the goods in display cases, and its chief rival at the time, Shirokiya, introduced shop girls in Western-style dresses. The department stores did not stoop to bargain like common street stalls. They held to a fixed schedule of listed prices.

From the beginning, the stores drew their crowds as much by culture and entertainment as they did by merchandise. The new fashions displayed in the Kabuki Theater or the floating world were instantly displayed. Today, they continue to draw crowds with special exhibits such as a "Spanish month", complete with a borrowed Goya or two. Many department stores hold rather elaborate art exhibitions, usually on a top floor so that the visitor has to pass through the rest of the store in order to get to it. One sees the announcements everywhere. The stores are usually willing to pay fairly large fees, which are often snapped up by financially strapped art museums in America and Europe.

Tokyo still bucks the world-wide trend that saw many famous inner city establishments close down or move to suburban malls. They continued to thrive even as people moved out of the center of Tokyo. It may be that the scarcity of married women with careers meant that matrons had more time to ride into the city center to shop. And, of course, the transportation links are superb. Five railway lines converge in Ginza, bringing half a million shoppers a day. On Sunday the main thoroughfare is closed and turned into a pedestrian mall. As the booming 80s gave way to the more frugal 90s, however, the stores began to see a decline in sales. And then, something truly remarkable happened.

"Cheap, cheap, cheap," blares a voice over a loudspeaker like a street merchant hawking fish and vegetables. The edges of the store are fringed with small red flags announcing deep discounts. These are words not normally heard in Ginza, which boasts not only the world's most expensive real estate but also many of its most fashionable shops. Ginza was moving down market. More than a few heads turned when the upstart retailer from Hiroshima, Goro Aoyama, opened a discount men's store one block from Ginza's main shopping street, just around the corner from the proud Matsuya department store. Many retailers were shocked that he would open his store just as Japan's post-Bubble recession was gathering steam. But the inauguration turned out to be a public relations masterstroke. Newspapers and television stations had a field day reporting the thousands of salarymen who showed up for the grand opening, drawn by specials on suits for less than $20. Aoyama Trading Company and its founder became nationally famous overnight for prospering in the middle of a recession when virtually every other major department store chain was reporting steep declines in sales and profits. Customers that used to frequent designer boutiques flocked to the new store, happy to buy a standard suit at a reasonable price.

Suits now sell for more than $20 but not too much more. Most can be had for less than $300, about half the cost in a mainline store. The customers seem to be predominantly men, or perhaps a few women shopping for their husbands, happy enough to buy a suit with an obscure label at a reasonable price. Look elsewhere for Ralph Laurent polo shirts, Burberry raincoats, or Jean Paul Gaultier dresses. The merchandise at Aoyama Trading Company is pretty basic: suits, mostly in dark colors, sport coats, also in dark colors, and trousers. Piles of plain white shirts made in Indonesia go two for $30. In short, the basic salaryman's uniform. Aoyama says he didn't want the average customer spending a month's salary to buy a suit, and one doesn't have to at his stores. None of this has been lost on the traditional giants, most of who now offer basic suits at more reasonable prices along with their Armani suits and Turnbull & Sasser dress shirts.

Of course, brand names and luxury never totally went out of fashion. Even during the decade of stagnant growth and intermittent recession, plenty of people in Tokyo spent a lot of money on luxury goods. Many women in their 30s and 40s, especially those in successful careers, were happy to lay out $5,000 on a Hermes "Kelly" handbag (named after the late American film actress Grace Kelly). For them it was an ultimate status symbol, and it was cheaper than a luxury car or a deluxe home. So popular were the bags that some buyers had to wait six months to get one. Gucci prayed for similar success with its "Jacki-O Bag", one American icon pitted against another. No luxury goods maker could afford to ignore Japan's market. In 1999, Hermes opened a new outlet in Ginza, next door to the Sony Building. During the remodeling, the building was shrouded in distinctive Hermes orange, making it look like a gift box.

A person can work up quite a lather hiking around the Ginza district on a hot summer day. To cool off, just drop ¥110 in a curbside machine and pick up a can of Pocari Sweat. In no city in the world are there so many vending machines. The humble automated merchants can be seen everywhere, even in the most fashionable shopping districts. By last count there were more than five million of them in Japan, and surely a large portion of them must be in the capital, usually with a nearby receptacle overflowing with discarded cans and container boxes. The variety of things that can be purchased from a Tokyo vending machine is astonishing. Besides the usual cigarettes, soft drinks and canned coffee, the unmanned emporiums sell rice, fruit, comic books, pornography, underwear, disposable cameras, flowers, personalized business cards and alcoholic beverages, not merely cans of beer but whole bottles of vodka and fifths of whiskey.

It is surprising to see beer and hard liquor so openly and readily available. Virtually every liquor store in the capital seems to have one or two of these automated barmen ready to serve up a nightcap on holidays or after closing time. It is testimony to the country's orderliness that these machines can be left unattended on public streets without being broken into or vandalized. It is also testimony to a certain callous indifference to the underage drinking laws that has caused them to come under attack of late from both local groups and even the World Health Organization. The Ministry of

Health and Welfare is moving to shut them down and insist that sales of alcoholic beverages be made only on a face-to-face basis.

But mostly they sell a bewildering variety of soft drinks, coffee and elixirs. That latter is a peculiar kind of energizer that hard-working Japanese buy from vending machines or station kiosks when they feel in need of a quick pick-me-up. Here are a few of the other concoctions offered for sale: Fruipy, Genki Ghurt, Dydo, Vegetake, Yogurina Soda, Calpis Water, Blendy, Air, Acerola, CappuCcino, Jive Coffee, Plain White Water ("with a gallon of deliciousness in every drop"), Super Triath, Grapefruit Tea, Post Water ("it moistures your body and softens your soul"), Black Lemon, Vitamin Water, Eau + V, and Yordy Light. Many of the purveyors evidently feel that Tokyo people are woefully deficient in ions. Hence Ion Support and the appealingly-named SPO-ENEC100 and Wilson, which the makers are proud to declare is made with "Oligo, which activates the bio-fido-bacterium that adjusts yours body."

What the consumer buys, he usually discards in short order. Tokyo's people are waste makers of the first magnitude. Department stores encourage customers to discard the old and buy the new. Each season when new bathing suits appear, piles of the old-style suits must be jettisoned and carted off to land fills in Tokyo Bay. Makers of home appliances and furniture come out with slightly different, minutely improved models that their customers feel they must have, and, of course, the older models must be discarded to make room. Every year, Tokyoites junk furniture, television sets, bicycles, rice cookers by the hundreds of thousands. Many of the discards are in perfectly good working order, sometimes practically brand new.

It used to be that *gaijin*, or foreigners, living in Tokyo could outfit their entire apartments with the discards they found by roaming the back alleys on garbage collection days. It was a boon for missionaries, teachers and students and others living on tight budgets in the world's most expensive city. They could find television sets in good working order, refrigerators, microwave ovens and furniture of all kinds. The Japanese were too fastidious to do it themselves. Tokyo residents have to pay a small fee to have the larger stuff hauled away, and that has cut down the number of things that can be picked up for free. The sassy city magazine *Tokyo Journal*, aimed at the expatriate community, lamented, "the Tokyo staple, the color television set, is on the endangered species list." Still, it went on, and there are a few happy hunting grounds left. The Denenchofu district is a good place to look for expensive clothing and the occasional discarded work of art. The Ikebukuro district is said to be the best place to hunt for refrigerators, air conditioners, heaters and other home electrical appliances. The Shinjuku East district is the graveyard for discarded bicycles, while a trip into suburban Saitama prefecture can yield the occasional television set.

There is another way for citizens to get good free stuff from the garbage pile. The Bureau of Sanitation maintains five centers where large but workable discards are handed out by lot. Television sets, microwave ovens, desks, kitchen tables and chairs have all been cleaned, repaired and displayed with numbers attached to them. Anyone can apply for up to two items. After a two-week viewing period, the department sends the winner a post card. Each center also publishes a newsletter filled with free ads of people looking to unload or pick up specific kinds of used articles.

The garage sales like those held in America to clear the home of unwanted junk are unknown in Tokyo. Of course, there isn't much space on which to display wares, and it is probably too personal for Japanese to spread their used appliances or old clothes for neighbors to see. For the older generation, it may also bring back painful memories of the dark days after World War II when many people had to sell personal valuables just to buy food. The spirit of frugality that swept through Japan in the backwash of the Bubble Era, however, has brought back the flea market. In Tokyo, large markets are organized every Sunday in virtually any large open space, parks, parking lots and sporting fields. At the most popular location in downtown, Yoyogi Park vendor space is allocated by lot, so only one out of three applicants is usually lucky enough to spread his or her wares out in a six-square meter spot. Everything seems for sale: faded army jackets, food-stained baby clothes, frayed comic books, worn-out eating utensils. Most Sundays will find thousands of people rediscovering the pleasures of face-to-face haggling. The Citizens Recycling Society, which organizes many of these events, tried to arrange the first flea markets in the early 1980s and failed. Ten years later, they were the rage.

Some of the items on sale at these flea markets may have been obtained as gifts. Japanese have an exaggerated penchant for giving and receiving presents, but it reaches a frenzied pitch twice a year. During *oseibo*, the end of the year, and, at *ochugen*, midsummer, people give presents to fellow workers, relatives or business associates. Mainline department stores derive no small part of their annual profits from these sales, since great importance is attached to the wrapping that the present comes in. The names Mitsukoshi and Takashimaya still denote quality and style. Whole floors of these stores are given over to extravagant displays of gift packages. Yet it can be an extraordinary wasteful habit. It is, after all, not enough to merely send a gift-carton of cookies. Each individual biscuit must be wrapped individually, placed in its own plastic-molded tray and put inside a wooden or tin box. The box is then wrapped in the store's own distinctive paper and presented to the customer in a plastic shopping bag.

Often, no real thought is given to the tastes or preferences of the receiver. Non-drinkers are saddled with expensive bottles of whiskey, housewives get more cooking oil or instant coffee than they can possibly use in a year. In the houses of more prominent Tokyoites, whole rooms are set aside to store all of the unwanted stuff until it can be used or given away to needier relatives. Sometimes they furtively sell the gifts to merchants who ply the backstreets of the city's wealthier districts and then resell them to pawnshops. But many of them are simply thrown in the trash and added to the landfill in Tokyo Bay.

It is impossible to walk around Tokyo without having things thrust in your hands constantly. Girls stand outside of the railroad stations handing out small packages of tissue with advertisements on them. Demonstrators hand you their bill of grievances — never mind that you are a foreigner and can't do anything to set the problem right. Wander into the post office to mail a letter, and they will be celebrating the 100th anniversary of rural delivery and will hand you a gift bag filled with a commemorative pen, a soft drink and a pamphlet. The smallest art exhibit is incomplete without providing every patron with a printed biography of the artist and a four-color brochure illustrating his previous work and maybe a small gift. Even that great promoter of waste reduction, the Tokyo Metropolitan Government, evidently feels that people cannot cross its new Rainbow Bridge on foot without the aid of two full-color brochures. One day's haul can fill a good-sized satchel: eight packs of pocket-sized boxes of tissue, a sample of a new shampoo, three "vitamin" candies attached to flyers for a loan company, a breath mint sample, a large pamphlet extolling the virtues of Akita prefecture, several applications for a credit card, and a couple packages of chewing gum.

The annual Tokyo *Gomi Shukai*, a trash rally, fills city hall and the citizen's plaza with booths representing various recycling companies. Skits on the outdoor stage emphasize the need to cut down the volume of garbage. An exhibition of paintings gives children's perspectives of the problem and offers brochures about metal compacting or pamphlets about waste paper recycling. Everyone plies visitors with paper circulars, pamphlets, brochures or boxes of tissue paper and rolls of toilet paper made from recovered waste paper. There is nothing to do but either haul the stuff around the city, or, after checking that nobody is watching, toss it all in the trash.

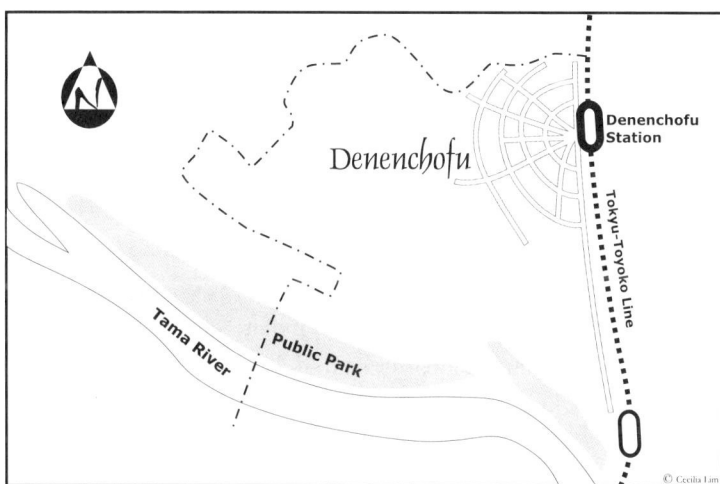

## Tokyo's Beverly Hills

In Tokyo, it is almost as hard to find a truly rich neighborhood as it is to uncover a genuine slum. There are, of course, subtle gradations. Certainly a Sanbancho or an Azabu address speaks of substance, just as Sanya passes for Tokyo's skid road. Neighborhoods such as Hiroo cater to foreigners on the kind of fat expatriate allowances that allow them to live in spacious, American-style apartments in the crowded capital. For the most part, however, the wealthy live in close proximity with the — well, less wealthy. It is hard to find any real poverty in the city. As often as not, the bank manager may live on the same street as the bank teller, possibly even taking the same subway to work every day.

A notable exception is the Denenchofu neighborhood in the western part of the capital. It might be called Tokyo's Beverly Hills, except that the homes there, though substantial to be sure, are hardly mansions in the Western sense of the word. Indeed, they would hardly be out of place in any better off neighborhood in a North American city with sidewalks, tree-lined streets and comfortable though unostentatious residences set back from the street. Along the western side of Denenchofu lies a pleasant public park overlooking the Tama River. Where the river makes a bend, an elderly man has set up an easel and is sketching the scene. On the alluvial plain, another man is practicing golf shots. The park grounds are golden in the late autumn with fallen ginko leaves.

Unlike most Japanese neighbourhoods, Denenchofu has a recognizable pattern to it. The streets radiate outwards like spokes on a wheel in a circular pattern around a small town square. A variety of building styles can be discerned by walking along the pathways. Some homes look like Cape Cod houses in New England; others are built in more traditional Japanese styles with lovely, sculpted hedges and pine trees in the yard. The square itself has some fashionable shops, a German bakery and coffee shop and a very discreet Kentucky Fried Chicken outlet.

Denenchofu was Tokyo's first truly "planned" community, an anomaly in this largely unplanned, helter-skelter city. It was conceived in the 1920s, when city planners were gripped by the fashion for building "garden suburbs" to draw people from the overcrowded city centers. *Denen* means "pastoral" in Japanese. Its patron was none other than Eiichi Shibusawa, the tycoon who is sometimes called the "father of Japanese capitalism." The first plots went on sale in 1923, a propitious year since the Great Kanto Earthquake, which devastated the older eastern part of the city along the Sumida River, hastened the movement of people to the west towards the Tama River. Even today it has its own community association with more than the usual number of rules controlling, say, the height of the homes (no more than two stories.) or the amount of land that can be built on.

The initial land prices were far from cheap, but they were within the means of the upper middle classes. Denenchofu attracted mostly professionals, university professors, lawyers and the like. The Bubble Era pushed land prices to extraordinary levels just about the time when the first generation was passing on, so their heirs had to cope with paying huge inheritance taxes. Some could not cope and were forced to sell, and their places have been taken in some instances by nouveau riche owners of property companies and celebrities, including a few film or television personalities.

The residents are proud of their history — a concrete plaque explaining the background graces the town's square — and fiercely protect their reputation. Posted on the notice board at the bus stop is a community newsletter complaining about the proliferation of neighborhoods in other Japanese cities that want to appropriate the name. A delegation from Fukushima in northern Honshu wants to name its posh new subdivision Denenchofu. The request is turned down. "Don't allow copy-name towns," the newsletter declares.

— T.C.

# 4

# People

On the east side of the Imperial Palace is a part of Tokyo rich with the ambiance of old Edo. Portions of the Kanda district lay within the outer defense perimeter of the shogun's castle, but the real spirit of the community always was in the low-lying plebeian districts further in, known as *shitamachi*. It was here that the craftsmen and artisans who built the castle settled in neighborhoods that were often demarked by craft — carpenters here, dyers there. It was a district full of markets and temples. The gaudy Akihabara electronics center is still a magnet for tourists, even though it is slowly losing customers to the new discount stores in Shinjuku and the suburbs. For many years, the Kanda district was synonymous with second-hand bookstores. Students from the several nearby universities provided them with steady customers for decades. Many bookstores remain but they struggle against rising rents. The universities themselves, some of them at least, are also picking up and moving to the exurbs.

Bustling Yasukuni-dori is Kanda's main thoroughfare. During the day, its sidewalks teem with young people shopping for ski clothes and snowboards among the numerous sporting goods emporiums that line the street. For many years, one of the landmarks along Yasukuni Street was the Heiwa-do (Peace) Shoe store, owned by the family of Kunio Saso, who traces his ancestry back to the former *samurai*, or warrior, Junichiro Hisanori Saso. After the feudal system was abolished with the Meiji Restoration of 1868, samurai like Saso were set adrift and had to find new ways of making a living. Junichiro laid down his twin swords and became a judo instructor. But it was his enterprising wife Chiyo who founded the family fortune, the shoe factory, later to become a store. Under their adopted son Mohei, Heiwa-do flourished in the 1920s, as the Japanese embraced the new fashion for Western-style clothes. It introduced modern refinements such as open display windows, concrete floors, chairs for customers to sit on while they tried on shoes, all of which was novel at the time. Destroyed in the American fire-bombing raids in early 1945, Heiwa-do re-opened at its familiar corner in 1955. Kanda still bustles with people, at least by day. The bookstores still draw browsers by the hundreds. Yet the rising land values of the late 1990s forced some universities to move to less expensive areas on the outskirts of Tokyo. The population is changing also, as more people move out of what might elsewhere be called the "inner city," to the far-lying suburbs. Change eventually caught up with the Heiwa-do store, too. The familiar two-story building was torn down and replaced with a stylish, steel and glass edifice with some stately red-granite trim. The shoe store occupies the first two floors, while the upper stories are rented to other tenants.

It seems like everywhere one looks in Kanda construction is under way. Older wooden houses have long given way to concrete mansion-type apartments, and smaller neighborhood shops to office buildings and retail chains. Everywhere steel skeletons are draped in blue canvas, a sure sign that a new building is being erected. Saso points out a small vacant lot being used as a temporary parking lot. "The owner would like to build on it, but his neighbors won't sell." The parking business flourished after the Bubble Economy burst. Landowners leased their idle properties to parking lot operators in hopes of covering at least part of their taxes and the interest on the loans that they took out during the boom years. Everywhere can be seen the ubiquitous "pencil" buildings. These are office buildings or apartments of eight or ten stories that are built on a narrow plot of land, only a meter or two separating them one from another. The tight, round stairways on the outside banister gives the effect of being a pencil, or perhaps the binding on a spiral notebook.

Kanda was never a center for corporate headquarters, despite its proximity to the city's financial center and its excellent transportation connections, but that may be changing too. Mitsui Marine Insurance Co. has moved its corporate headquarters to a large building where Chuo University used to have its campus. The university moved to suburban Hachioji a few years back. But no major department stores have relocated to Kanda, and fewer of the small grocery stores and other local amenities that used to be a pillars of neighborhood life here since Edo times can be seen. They have been taken over by purveyors of upscale sportswear and snow skis for fashionable young people, who are drawn from all parts of the city, giving the district a youthful ambiance.

Saso points out another family enterprise, the Inagawa-ro bathhouse, its solid, gray concrete and black chimney looking a little out-of-place among the modern sportswear shops. The lettering on the front proudly proclaims that the original building was erected on this site in Meiji 2 (1870). It survived the Great Kanto Earthquake and the American bombing attacks in World War II. In its heyday, at least 300 people used to visit and bathe there every day. To be sure, not as many homes had their own private baths as do today. More than that, though, the Inagawa-ro was a focal point of the neighborhood life, a center for socializing. By the end of the 1980s, however, fewer than 50 people were showing up, and many of them were older people who had not yet moved to the suburbs. In March 1992, the 122-year-old Inagawa-ro, the oldest in Tokyo, closed its doors for the last time.

*Sento*, or public baths, are steeped in the history and tradition of Edo as old as the city itself. The first sento opened in 1591, only a year after Ieyasu Tokugawa moved his capital to Edo. Soon every neighborhood had one, instantly recognizable by a tell-tale chimney. Over the centuries, they have served as centers of community life, sort of like pubs in London or general stores in old New England. It was a place where neighbors came, not just to get clean, but also meet other people and pass the time. Of course, at the time indoor plumbing was rare even in Tokyo. As late as the 1960s, many households were without their own baths. And those that had them were small and cramped, so people still went to the baths, handing over ¥300 to ¥500 to the *bandai-san* sitting on the raised dais, collecting their towel and heading off to the baths, men on one wide of a partition, women on the other.

The bather sits down on a wooden (these days it's probably plastic) stool in front of a small spigot and washes himself with soap or shampoo. Only after he has thoroughly rinsed by pouring water over the head and body with a bucket, does he climb into the large communal tub for a long soak in water heated to 39 or 40 degrees Celsius, some of which, even in Tokyo, bubbles up from natural hot springs. Until recently, it was considered obligatory for people to visit the sento on New Year's Day for a ritual purification. It was an act hearkening back to the days when bathing was associated with purity and baths were located in Shinto shrines.

Public bath houses have been closing almost every week in Tokyo, victims of changing habits, growing affluence and the rising value of land beneath them, which makes it almost imperative that owners convert them into something more profitable. The sento reached its apogee in the 1960s, when private baths were still something of a rarity. In 1968 nearly 2,700 sento were open in Tokyo. At the end of the 1990s, the number had fallen to about 1,400. Aficionados work hard to keep them from dying off entirely. Some ward offices provide the elderly with bathing coupons, and some have even begun to underwrite the operating costs. The Tokyo Metropolitan Government subsidizes a bi-monthly magazine *1010*, pronounced as *sen to* in Japanese, to try and maintain interest in the tradition. The Sento Club, formed under the auspices of the Tokyo Bath Union and comprised of individuals ranging from company presidents to taxi drivers, picks a new sento to soak in every month. "We are all different ages, we all have different jobs, but when we're in the bath naked, we're all the same," says club president Takehiko Sugita.

To lure customers, some sento owners are converting their establishments into urban "health spas," complete with saunas, massage, fitness equipment, karaoke, plus a mind-boggling array of the latest techno-health gimmicks. Typical of these newer water pleasure palaces is Yutopia (*yu* means hot water in Japanese) near the railway station in Okigubo, a bedroom community on the Chuo line. Gone is the traditional bandai-san, taking fares from his raised dais. Patrons enter a foyer that looks more like the lobby of a modest hotel (which in a way is what it is; one can stay all night for an extra fee.) The entrance fee is ¥2,000, is considerably higher than the ¥500 or so charged at a more traditional neighborhood bath. The male patron picks up his locker key and heads to the fourth floor baths. Women are on the second floor.

Not one bath, but several. They come in every permutation one can imagine. At the center is one that might be called the "normal" bath with a nice 40°c temperature. Next to it, a man soaks blissfully in another pool cooled to 16 degrees. The urban spas vie with each other to present the most unusual baths. Yutopia's include a germanium bath, a cypress bath and a mugwart steam sauna. The Yuupurza in Edogawa Ward boasts a milk bath, while Kurhaus in Ota Ward offers no fewer than 13 different varieties, including a wet sauna, a dry sauna and a body steamer, all filled with water pumped from a natural underground spring. Everything one could possibly need for personal hygiene, tooth brushes, hair brushes, plastic razors, and nail clippers, are available for the taking from plastic buckets.

Drained of energy after a long soak, the patron puts on his "relaxation wear," a light green, short-sleeved shirt and short pants, and pads over to the darkened television room, where he flops down on comfortable low-reclining easy chairs in the semi-darkness. At one end of the room are the flickering lights of a large TV set broadcasting a sumo match. Most of the men, semi-comatose, snore. Energy restored, they may repair upstairs, where they can have a meal at the restaurant- cafeteria whose menu might typically offer spaghetti, sushi and *soba*, or buckwheat noodles. Professional masseuses are available for those wanting an old fashioned rubdown. One can sit in a large vibrating easy chair, heads bowed under the plastic hood, listening to the trilling of bird songs and breathing deeply of the "scent-of-the-day." After that, thoroughly relaxed, the bathhouse patron is ready to meet the rigors of home and the next-day's work.

By day, Kanda is teeming with young people, but relatively few of them live there now. For many of those left behind, Kanda has become a rather lonely place. Mrs. Kinoshita, 82, has lived in the same house for 43 years. A widow for the last twenty years, her only regular companion is her cat Sabu. It seemed like before she knew it, her familiar surroundings had changed beyond recognition. The vegetable store closed, and so did the fish store. "I don't like the evenings because everybody is going back to their family. It's very painful when there is nobody to talk to." Her sister lives farther west in Itabashi, but Mrs. Kinoshita has given no thought to moving there. "I've lived here a long time and feel comfortable. Also, my husband is here," she says, looking at a picture of her husband Kenjiro.

A sign that reads 'Mikawa Pastry Shop' still hangs in front of the shop that Kikutaro Sato, 83, ran for 62 years. Inside, the menu is still visible among the clutter of tables, chairs and scattered magazines. Sato and his wife had worked in the shop from 5 a.m. until well after dark. "Sometimes it was hard, but most of the time, it was enjoyable," he recalls. A year ago the shop closed. A rent rise proved to be too much to bear. "It's not only our store but the vegetable store and the fruit store. Ours was one of the last ones on the street to close." Now the Satos are planning to move in with their daughter's family in suburban Saitama prefecture. "I never thought we would have to move to a new place in our old age. We both had planned to live here in Kanda until we died."

During the Bubble Era, many residents were bullied out of their homes by shadowy thugs — "land sharks" — from Japan's underworld, once a lucrative side business of the *yakuza*, or gangsters. They were hired by developers to intimidate reluctant property owners into selling up and moving out. When one owner of a small laundry refused an offer to sell his small holding, he began hearing ominous noises from the empty apartment next door. When he still didn't take the hint, things got rougher. He awoke early one morning to the sound of crashing and tearing in the shop below. Downstairs a four-ton truck was grinding back and forth among the racks of clothing. "All because I wouldn't move out," he lamented. Fending off these hoodlums became something of a way of life for many residents of the older sections of Tokyo. Strangers would come by in the early morning and bang on the doors and shout. Or, they moved into vacant apartments and played loud music or even loudly chanted Buddhist sutras well into the early morning hours. In the extreme, they might poke holes in the roof of the buildings or resort to arson. Those who successfully resisted often found it to be an empty victory. The holdout inevitably discovered that his tiny house or shop was surrounded by cold office buildings, the local sushi shop had disappeared to be replaced by a ski emporium, the public bath had closed, and all the faces on the street were those of utter strangers.

Most families, however, didn't need the prod of yakuza to persuade them to sell out. The inevitability of death and the certainty of the inheritance tax were usually incentives enough. This tax, enacted in 1905 as a means of preventing the accumulation of excessive wealth in families, can run as high as 70 percent of the value of the land and property and is due in cash within one year. With property values bloated by the speculation that swept through the city in the 1980s, many survivors faced tax bills that ran into the millions of yen, certainly not something to give the family head peace of mind in his golden years. The usual solution, of course, was to sell the homestead and put the proceeds into a modest apartment building or an office complex. That is what Saso did with the family bath house and venerable shoe store. The taxes on these properties would come to more than a million dollars. And, as he puts it, "we can't get that by selling shoes." Those who waited until the bubble burst were caught in a double bind. They faced stiff taxes based on the inflated value of the land but had a hard time finding anyone who wanted to buy it. Some in that situation were driven to extremes. In 1993, a couple in their 60s ended it all when they were presented with a $2 million bill on the land they had inherited in Denenchofu. They tried to sell the land to raise money to pay the tax but found few takers in the property slump and after receiving a final notice, the pair committed suicide by taking poison.

Kinji Kubo, who owns a small construction company in Kanda, is a crusader for preserving the community spirit. From a feeling of community duty, Kubo publishes several magazines and picture books of the district, and as a hobby he also prints "treasure hunting" maps, detailing Kanda's famous bridges, statues and temples. They are distributed widely to school children to teach them about their home. "The older people here still feel a sense of community, but not so much the younger generation," he says somewhat sadly. There are no longer enough local people to make up the popular Kanda-Myojin shrine festival, although, he adds, many younger people from outside Kanda, who enjoy helping to keep these popular festivals going, fill out the ranks. "It's very difficult to keep up a sense of community spirit here." Then on reflection, he adds, "the important thing is to try to keep Kanda livable, because so many people are moving to other places."

*Machi zukuri*, or community building, was one of Tokyo's buzz words in the 1990s. It covered a host of volunteer activities, some of them run by local ward governments, others by private groups. Of course, Japanese have bonded together in groups and associations for generations, but the idea of volunteering is relatively new. It really began to expand following the 1995 earthquake that devastated Kobe. Dozens of volunteer groups descended on that city, performing services that the government did not to provide. Every ward now has a center that serves as a clearinghouse and matching service for groups and individuals wanting to volunteer and those needing their services. Monthly calls go out for volunteers for such diverse projects as a well-digging expedition to Bangladesh or fresh air mountain trips for mentally challenged adults. The Tokyo Metropolitan Government now appropriates eight percent of its budget to something called "welfare," which covers everything from day-care (still somewhat limited) to home helpers for the elderly.

Members of the Hydrangea Volunteer Group meet every Wednesday at the Minato Ward Volunteer Center to prepare and deliver meals to elderly residents who have registered for the service. They work in two details: cooks and deliverers. The cooks, six women ranging in age from 35 to 50, begin preparing the day's ration of 36 meals at 10:30 a.m. The six volunteer deliverers — at an average age of 70, most of them are eligible to be recipients — arrive at noon to pick up the meals and then head out on foot, bicycle or car. The Hydrangea is one of a growing number of small volunteer groups sponsored and coordinated by the city's extensive network of volunteer centers.

The Shinjuku District Volunteer Center monthly newsletter includes, among others, requests from a 75-year old man who wants somebody to walk with him to a local *go* parlor, a place where people play the board game of *go*, and a 39-year old man in wheelchair who just started to live alone. He describes himself as a "cheerful pro-wrestling fan" looking for someone to come over to his house to visit. There seems to be a group devoted to every imaginable, and some quite unimaginable, activity. The Egg Association seeks members interested in the homeless problem. However, they do not seek to help the homeless by offering food or clothing, but seek to "study" the problem by talking to homeless people. Their subjects were initially reluctant to talk — no surprise there — so the group decided to distribute hard-boiled eggs in exchange for conversation, hence the name.

A Minato group meets once a month to clothe a meter-high replica of Brussels' Mannekin Pis statue, who does his business at the far end of the Yamanote line platform at Hamamatsucho Station. The volunteers make season-appropriate costumes for the normally nude boy and change his outfits once a month. In December he is dressed as Santa Claus; in January he wears a costume of the animal of the new year on the Chinese calendar; and, so on. In 1999, his rabbit costume made him a dead ringer for the Easter bunny.

Most groups, however, like the Hydrangea Group, perform more traditional volunteer activities, but even then, the tasks are performed in a decidedly Japanese fashion. Cooks, working in an immaculate kitchen in traditional lunch-lady gear of hair nets and face masks are supervised by a dietician to ensure a nutritious lunch under 600 calories. The end product is a gorgeous *bento* box, a lunch box made of split bamboo, with grilled salmon, steamed vegetables, pickles, rice, miso soup and fresh strawberries for dessert — a lunch that would cost at least $15 in a department store gourmet shop. One social worker on the staff of the Minato Ward Volunteer Center admits that the efforts to educate the public are only just beginning. "What the Hydrangea Group and other groups are doing is good, but the scale is so small that I sometimes wonder if it makes a difference. We need to expand and to organize efforts in other areas too. One of the real problems is that even though we offer an extensive array of programs and opportunities, it is not much good if people don't know we are here." The Hydrangea volunteers themselves confirm that: "Until a friend told me about this I had no idea this kind of opportunity existed in Tokyo." It's a well-kept secret, unfortunately.

All of Tokyo's inner wards have been losing population for many years. Lately, they have been doing so at an accelerating pace. Many local authorities are obsessed with finding ways to stem the exodus. The English-language newsletter published by Minato Ward carries a population box on the lower right-hand corner of the front page as if it were taking the ward's vital signs. The prognosis is not good. In one edition the population was reported to be 154,683, a decrease of 1,027 from the previous month, although the foreign-born population had increased by about 200 people during the same period. Taito Ward was the first to try to stem the flow by offering young families rent subsidies. Up to $385 a month was available to families with children, provided that they stayed in the ward. Most of the other wards in central Tokyo have adopted similar programs or other schemes that link requirements for providing residential housing with new commercial developments.

As the population and birthrate continue to shrink, local authorities have had to consider closing or consolidating schools. Many of them are venerable institutions. The Tomoe Primary School in Toranomon, the oldest public school in Japan, closed its doors after 120 years. "We are very sorry that our school will disappear," the principal, Minegishi Morio, told reporters. The *Asahi Evening News* ran a rather forlorn picture of Sakamoto Primary School near the Tokyo Stock Exchange. It showed the school's new intake — all six of them — neatly lined up in chairs at the opening assembly, their parents sitting behind them. Chiyoda Ward, however, was the first to come up with a comprehensive restructuring program, which it said would help stem the exodus of residents by providing new public housing and cultural amenities while closing redundant schools. It called for the closing of six primary schools and two middle schools, many of them with proud histories. "We decided it would be best to overhaul the entire system at once," proclaimed the Chiyoda Mayor Kimura Shigeru.

The parents of Bancho Elementary School in Kojimachi, one of the oldest and most prestigious schools in Tokyo, were not about to give up without a fight. Technically, Bancho was not slated for demolition. But as far as the parents were concerned, they might as well have brought in the wrecking ball. Japanese don't invest much emotion in physical structures and ivy-covered halls. There is nothing physically remarkable about Bancho School. It is a four-story, reinforced-concrete structure, like hundreds of others all over Japan. No, a school's heritage of emotion is bound up in its proud name, its long history, its school song and flag — all of which were to change. What upset many parents was not so much that the building might or might not be torn down but that the school would be consolidated with another and have to adopt a new name, new song, and a new flag — a whole new set of traditions. "Bancho's history will be finished," lamented one parent.

Certainly Bancho and the other schools in Chiyoda Ward are steeped in tradition. Many of them date back to the Meiji era when Japan opened its doors to the outside world and adopted such Western institutions as a parliament, a standing army and public schools. Shigeru Yoshida, Japan's great post-war prime minister, attended Bancho, novelist Soseki Natsume, author of **I Am a Cat**, attended Kinka primary school in Kanda. Chizakura elementary, also slated to be torn down, was built on the site of a renowned samurai school. Ryoma Sakamoto, who played an important role in setting the stage for the Meiji Restoration, was a graduate of that school. A well-known path to success is Bancho to Kojimachi Middle School, to Hibiya High School and finally, the ultimate, Tokyo University.

It is not hard, however, to see why the ward authorities felt the need to come up with such a plan. On the surface, Chiyoda Ward has all the attributes of a world-class city center. It has big buildings and broad avenues. The Diet and the main government ministries are here, as is the Marunouchi financial district. "Chiyoda-ku, Tokyo 100" is an address known far and wide. The national theater and the supreme court building are located along the palace moat. And, of course, at the very center, like a hole in the donut, is the vast emptiness of the Imperial Palace grounds. Every day more than a million people emerge from the numerous subway exits for the day's work. The trouble is that these same people all disappear back into the subways and ride home to the suburbs in the evening. In terms of its permanent population, Chiyoda is a mere town. Fewer than 40,000 people live there now, compared with 120,000 in 1956.

The local ward authorities feared that if the population continues to fall, Chiyoda might lose its sole member of the Tokyo Metropolitan Assembly — or worse, it might end up being consolidated with another ward. This is no small consideration; Chiyoda Ward was created by merging the old Kanda and Kojimachi Wards). It was inconceivable that the very heart of Tokyo might one day end up without a voice at city hall, and the ward seemed willing to spend a huge sum in order to prevent that from happening. An astonishing $700 million was budgeted for the project, which involved building new apartments and culture centers on old school sites and even turning some existing schools into high-rise buildings. The goal, the ward said, was to increase and stabilize the population at around 50,000. The Bancho parents are unimpressed. "I've counted up the new residents, and they only come to about 600 new units," parent Kenji Sugimura claimed. They were also suspicious of the ward's real intentions. The proposal would, after all, open up several attractive building sites in the most desirable part of the city. Nagatacho primary school next to Japan's parliament hill, one of the schools slated to be torn down, was designated an 'empty site' on the ward's plans. The plot was about 1,200 *tsubo* in size, about 35,000 square feet, when one tsubo in central Tokyo was worth about ¥100 million. "Every developer in Japan is watching it closely." The ward is controlled by the Liberal Democratic Party, whose need for campaign funds seem to be bottomless and whose connections with the construction industry are impeccable. The Nagatacho School is located conveniently close to the headquarters of the LDP. Would the LDP be able to profit in some unfathomable way from the redevelopment projects? The question was not unreasonable in light of the money scandals that would later dog the LDP. Nevertheless, Chiyoda Ward was determined to proceed with the redevelopment project. "We acknowledge that this [protest] action shows the love and concern that parents have for Chiyoda and their own schools," said the planning department's Mohoko Taniguchi. "But it is definitely necessary to proceed if we think of the future of the ward in light of the declining population," she added.

The parents launched a petition drive to prevent the school's closure and even tried to recall the ward mayor, a legitimate but fairly rare exercise in local Japanese politics. Saso was deeply involved in the campaign. The mayor narrowly survived the recall vote, but Bancho School remained open under its own name. Across town the Nagatacho school was shut down, but the sale of the land is still tied up in law suits. Five other schools were closed. "We got one victory," said Saso later. "I'm very proud."

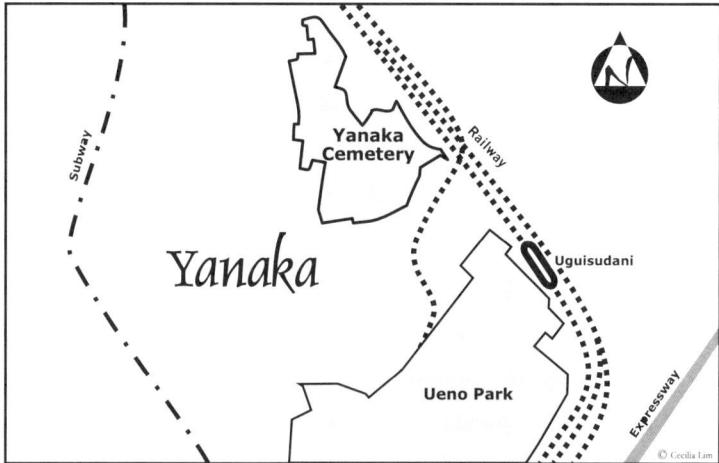

© Cecilia Lim

## Everything Old Is New Again

For about 15 years, until 1993, Takao Itoh worked as an engineer for a Swiss firm's Tokyo office. His business often took him to Europe, where he noticed and admired how historic buildings were lovingly preserved and converted for modern, practical use. An old house became a cafe, a stable was turned into a craft shop; or an abandoned but architecturally interesting warehouse saw new life as a night club. In Tokyo, such preservation and remodeling is rare.

Itoh had more than just a passing interest. He is the fifth generation owner of a building in Yanaka, in the *shitamachi* district, the "downtown" of today's Tokyo which was the low lands of old Edo where artisans, artists, musicians and common folk lived. From the mid-18th century until 1940 his family had owned and operated a pawnshop in the same location. The current building, built in 1847 along with a three-story warehouse building built in 1917, survived the Great Earthquake of 1923, the bombing in 1945, as did most of the area, and numerous neighbourhood fires. Though the buildings were too old for the family to live in, Itoh was reluctant to tear them down. He felt that they should be preserved and was searching for something to do with them. He remembered what he had seen in Europe and he knew what he would do: turn the former pawnshop into an art gallery.

Itoh opened his gallery, Space Oguraya, in 1994, first displaying watercolors painted by his then 81-year-old mother. They depicted scenes from Meiji Era Tokyo, painted from her memory. His timing was perfect. At just about the same time, shitamachi began to experience something of a renaissance. Crafts people, writers, designers and other arty types were starting to rediscover the charms of the old area. Shops opened selling handmade Japanese paper (*washi*), baskets and pottery. Galleries appeared in converted buildings, one of the largest and most successful in an old public sento.

Yanaka had always attracted visitors. The area has over 80 temples, a large cemetery and is close to Ueno Park, built in 1872. Old shopping streets sell homemade rice crackers, and a traditional Japanese house and garden, the home of sculptor Fumio Asakura, operates as museum. But the new shops added that extra cachet to the area, enough to attract the most coveted of all Tokyo's visitors: young working women with money to spend.

"Older people like to come to Yanaka from other parts of the city because it reminds them of the old days. The younger people like to come because it is somehow exotic to them. It's funny, but traditional Japanese culture is new to younger people in Tokyo. They've grown up surrounded by new, and for the most part, Western things. Rediscovering the old Tokyo has become fashionable," Itoh explained. Sure enough, as we sat talking in the gallery shop which occupies the former pawnshop front room, several groups of young women came through to look at the current exhibition of ink drawings of Tokyo by a local artist.

Preserving the old building wasn't Itoh's only motivation for opening the galley. "I wanted to add something to the community, to create a place where people could meet one another and artists could display their work in a comfortable, less formal setting. So far, I'm happy with the way its going but my next step is to get more involved in the 'culture business,' maybe promoting traditional Japanese music concerts."

Later, walking around the area myself, I saw several groups of young women having cake and tea at antique-filled coffee shops, buying ceramics and admiring temples. Yet despite the visitors, Yanaka remains a quiet Tokyo neighborhood; gentrification has hardly taken over. For every new quaint "old" shop, there are two Seven-Elevens, a dry cleaner and a run-down sandal shop. But it does have an unmistakable small-town Japan feel, rare in the rest of Tokyo. At least three times as I was exploring in Yanaka, people spotted me and eager to try out their English, called out, "Hello!" and "Good Morning!" whatever the time of day.

— S.F.M.

# 5

# Style

One of the best places to feel the energy of Tokyo is from the window of a coffee shop looking down on Shibuya station. As the trains disgorge people by the thousands, they quickly fill the square. They come from everywhere, from Yokohama or the depths of suburban Saitama prefecture or even farther away, perhaps linking up with friends in front of the bronze statue of the faithful dog, Hachiko. The light turns green, and the mighty tide of students, office ladies, shoppers and freaks surges across the intersection and disappears up the corridors that radiate out from the station. Immediately behind them, the square is already filling up again waiting for the signal to change. It goes on like this all day and well into the evening, regular as a heart beat, which in a way is what it is. All of Shibuya pulses to a youthful beat.

Everything that is fashionable, stylish, youthful and with-it about Tokyo can be found in walking distance of the Shibuya station. Of course, pockets of fashion consciousness exist elsewhere in the city, from the boutiques of Daikanyama to the night spots of

Roppongi. New in-spots for shopping, pleasure or entertainment spring up constantly. One year it is Jiyugaoka, the next Ebisu. Still, Shibuya remains the epicenter of youth culture, which increasingly sets the style for almost everyone in Tokyo. It sometimes seems that everyone on the street here is under 19, as if a special permit was needed just to walk around and gawk if you happen to be 25 or older. Almost everything that grew out of popular culture in recent years, from the Tamagotchi electronic virtual reality pet game of the late 1990s to the popularity of dyed hair and platform shoes, was probably first tried out or sold along Shibuya's streets and alleys. It has even spawned an adjective: *shibuya-kei* which, when applied to almost any product or social phenomenon, seems to give it the teen seal of approval.

Here youth is catered to. The streets and alleys are lined with stores designed to appeal to youthful tastes. They are filled with T-shirts with psychedelic art on the front or pictures of the 1950s film icon James Dean. The young people amble along wearing contemporary Tokyo grunge. For the men, it's a patchwork of army surplus jackets and old clothes bought at flea markets. For the young women, it's an eclectic mix of wool-knit caps, satin skirts with camisoles, a Louis Vuitton back pack, and loose cotton socks clinging to their ankles with the aid of sock glue. Hair styles are a palette of browns, reds, yellows, blues and purples. Each girl clutches a mobile telephone in one hand (Three out of four teen age girls in Tokyo own one.) and her precious Filofax™ notebook filled with telephone numbers and sheets of postage-stamp-sized photo stickers of their friends in the other. The pictures come out of the instant photo machines, embellished with flowers, animals and other cute stuff.

Who is this Shibuya Girl? She is as young as 15 or 16, a high school girl — or *kogyaru* to use a late 1990s vogue word. Literally, kogyaru is a combination of the Japanese character for child, *ko* and the English word "gal," which is pronounced gyaru in Japanese. They come directly from school, still in uniform, to hang out in Shibuya and slurp ice cream cones, snack on cheap sushi or check out pictures of their favorite television stars at a photo boutique. Japan may be the only country left in the world where high school students wear sailor suit style uniforms. According to *The Japan Times*, 47 percent of girls regard the uniform as the most important criterion when selecting a high school to apply to. The uniform of a school in Shinagawa, a caramel-colored blazer, red or blue plaid skirt and ribbon tie, was deemed the classiest. Second-hand girls' school uniforms, which are said to exert powerful sexual appeal to some Japanese men, command high prices on the secondary market. Customers include older women wanting to look younger and more chic as well as men with school-girl fetishes.

As young women move into their twenties, they are likely to spend several years working in an office, where they become "OLs", or office ladies. They invariably earn less money than their male counterparts but get to keep more of it, since they typically live at home (but with their own private room), paying either a nominal rent or none at all, thus beating the high cost of housing in the capital. And if she spends a bundle on a designer dress from a boutique, it only takes a month or so of frugality before the next splurge. Many do not have the same career ambitions as men, so they don't feel the same compulsion to save or to put in long hours at the office after quitting time or to forgo holidays. *Nikkei Reports*, a travel industry magazine, estimates that the typical office lady goes abroad every other year. Where shall it be this year? Phuket in Thailand or the Gold Coast of Australia?

No smart entrepreneur safely underestimates the power of the Shibuya Girl to set fashion trends or to move markets. Women may not hold many influential places in corporate Japan, but those thirty-something female executives who can sense what the teenage girl wants are invaluable assets. Miho Sasaki was the one who first proposed the idea of printing multiple postage-stamp sized photos, creating the fabulously successful Print Club for Atlus Co. "I thought it would be fun to shoot a person's face and make the photo into tiny stickers," she recalled. Atlus sold 24,000 print machines on that notion. The machines have graduated from fad status into a youth necessity. Options for photo frames that change with the seasons and passing fancies allow teens to "pose with" Brad Pitt or, should they want to, the current prime minister. The latest hit, "Nail More," is a machine for printing designs on girls' fingernails.

Aki Maita dreamed up the Tamagochi electronic pet, the Walkman of the 1990s, for Bandai Co. By the end of the decade, the craze had all but died, and Bandai was searching for another fad to latch onto. Yuko Yamaguchi, the chief designer at Sanrio, helped to revive 'Hello Kitty', the ultra cute white and pink kitten, whose cloying image seems to be everywhere, even on credit cards, by aiming the products directly at high school girls. In 1998-99, Sanrio grossed a billion dollars on its products. Yamaguchi still does a lot of street research in Shibuya and Harajuku, talking with teenage girls and trying to uncover their latest dreams. Indeed, it is common to see pollsters prowling Shibuya, clip boards in hand, asking young women and some young men their opinions on this or that, or photographers and camera crews recording the latest far-out hair colors and dress styles.

Tokyo is a hot house for creating and nurturing trends, fads, and styles. Some of them, like radioactive elements, have brief half-lives; others have extraordinary staying power. Hello Kitty originated in the 1970s, languished in the 1980s and early 1990s and then took off again spectacularly, with some subtle finetuning in marketing and image-making. A symbiosis exists between the hip young women and a vast media, print and electronic, that seems to exist solely to tell them what to buy, what to wear, where to eat, where to go on a date or holiday. Many trends originate with female television celebrities, known as *tarento*. This curious Japanese-English word, derived from "talent", often describes a celebrity who has no discernible talent at all, other than a pretty face and a manager with a marketing strategy strong enough to attract a huge following among Japanese girls. In the 1990s, the most influential tarento were Seiko Matsuda and Namie Amuro. The latter, a singer, seemed to shoot off fads with machine-gun rapidity: everything from wearing brown lipstick and white, knee-high boots to the fashion, very obvious in the streets of Tokyo, for women to dye their black hair various shades of brown or chestnut. Many tarentos lead rather Bohemian lives, which the public follows avidly in gossip magazines but does not necessarily mimic. Matsuda publicly ditched her husband and took up a string of affairs in New York. But it was not so much the lifestyle they live, however, as the clothes or cosmetics they wear. When Amuro disclosed on TV, wearing a mini-skirt with fringes, that she was getting married, though pregnant, it seemed as if everyone was soon wearing mini-skirts with fur fringes. It did not set off a fad for getting pregnant before marriage, but it did make the *dekichatta kekkon*, the shotgun wedding, something to boast about rather than hide. A fad for sporting bar-code tattoos also spread rapidly after Amuro appeared on one of her television shows with one printed on her writs. It had the message: "I love you."

Magazine editors constantly seek out new trends, and when they find one, they home in on it with saturation coverage. And suddenly it explodes. Whatever the editors cover is soon to be emulated, making it the ubiquitous look around town. The power of these magazines can be awesome, even if fundamentally trivial. One consumer magazine ran an eight-page tribute to the Italian dessert called tiramisu. Pretty soon, it seemed that every food establishment in Tokyo, from the smallest soba shop to Kentucky Fried Chicken needed to serve up the dessert.

Probably no magazine caught the spirit of its time, understood yet also molded its readers better than *Hanako*, published by Magazine House from its crowded warren of offices next to the national Kabuki Theater in downtown Tokyo. The magazine burst onto the publishing scene in 1988 at the zenith of the Bubble Era. Defying doubters, it quickly gained 300,000 regular readers and for a time enjoyed a six-month waiting list for advertising space. With its distinctive *New Yorker*-ish art covers (each one painted by the same Australian artist), *Hanako* can be found everywhere in the capital, in railway kiosks and bookstores. It circulates exclusively in Tokyo. A separate issue is published for the Osaka, Kyoto region. Some stores on the Ginza display a dozen or so back issues on the theory that the advice contained inside has a long shelf life.

*Hanako* claims to have literally created the OL, the female counterpart to the salaryman. Of course, young women have long worked for a few years in offices, serving tea, making photo copies and performing other routine chores in otherwise male-dominated office society before getting married, which usually means giving up work or career. But *Hanako* was the first to give them an identity and, more to the point, recognize them as style setters and as a marketing force in their own right. Editor Koji Tomono bristles at the suggestion that his readers are anything like the freaks that one can see on a Sunday afternoon in Harajuku, their blue hair glistening, tottering along in 4-inch platform boots. The Hanako girl is basically conservative. She plans to get married some day. In the meantime, she wants to spend and eat well. And *Hanako* and other magazines are there to help. *Hanako* estimates that its typical reader is 26.7 years old and has roughly $350 a month in disposable income to spread around any way she chooses.

Flipping through *Hanako's* glossy pages reveals many prevailing attitudes and values. In many ways, the magazine reflects a liberating spirit. It might carry, for example, an article on how a single woman can buy a condominium, including details on how to approach a bank for a loan and which ones offer the best deal. But unlike similar publications aimed at American women, there are no articles on glass ceilings or sexual harassment. *Hanako* is purely and simply about consumption. It is an encyclopedia of consumption. In each issue are page after page of small photographs of clothes, boutiques, handbags, scarves, perfume, disc players, dresses, cosmetics, food — all described in small, bite-sized articles. During the Bubble Era, its readers demanded information on designer label clothes and ¥30,000 dinners for two at trendy foreign restaurants. One of its early successes was a special issue devoted entirely to Chanel products. Yet when the Bubble burst, *Hanako* deftly moved to reflect the new fashion, frugality. Out went stories on high-fashion items, in came articles on how to save money. In 1990, a typical issue might contain articles on how to buy art or a series about expensive boutiques in the Daikanyama district. Two years later, the lead article was "123 restaurants in Ginza where you can eat for ¥3,000."

In Tokyo, women usually set the pace; men follow clumsily behind. Go to a trendy restaurant or attend a popular concert. Most of the patrons will be women. Normally, it is the woman who chooses the restaurant or the vacation spot. The man's function is to follow along and pay the bill. In the 1990s, a new expression entered the language: the "Narita Divorce." Two people get married in a lavish and expensive ceremony and leave on a honeymoon to

Europe, Hawaii or some other exotic foreign destination. The new husband is totally at sea, unable to make the simplest choice in a restaurant or negotiate the complexities of checking into a hotel. The new bride, steeped in magazine lore and having probably already taken several trips abroad herself, takes over. Arguments break out, the husband's ego is wounded and the couple decides that maybe they were not exactly made for each other after all. On returning to Tokyo's international airport at Narita, they decide to go their separate ways.

Men, of course, are not entirely impervious to the passing styles and fashions. The Shibuya Girl has her male counterpart, ambling along Shibuya's streets wearing perhaps bright yellow jogging pants, a camouflage jacket over a baggy, turtle-neck, pink socks and tennis shoes. Perversely, the lingering economic recession tended to put more money in the pockets of some men in their late teens and early 20s. They took up the trend of becoming part-time workers, sort of the male counterpart to the OL, rather than following the normal salaryman's path into a large corporation. They are now called *freetas* a new word which combines the English word "free" with the German word "arbeiter", which had previously been borrowed and altered into Japanese as their word for part-time workers. As the young men gradually loosened up and sought more ways of enjoying life than work, sports wear and casual clothing began to define the men's look. And like women, men have their own celebrity role models. Pop singer Izamu may have sparked a new fad among some young men for plucking their eyebrows and wearing cosmetics. The fad was reinforced by Kazuyoshi Funaki, gold medal ski jumper in the 1998 Olympic Games, who was shown on television and in magazines with his sharply trimmed brows.

As with women, an array of magazines cater to the interests of men. Editor Kazuhiro Saito aims his glossy magazine, *Brutus*, he says, at that relatively small segment of men who are aggressive consumers, but he admits that about 40 percent of the readers of this men's magazine are women. Like *Hanako* and other magazines, *Brutus* is obsessed with details. It has devoted whole issues to, say wine or sushi or some more esoteric topics. Whenever the Japanese male gets hooked on something, he becomes obsessed about it. He spends money on the things he loves most and wants to know everything about it. When vintage jeans (manufactured in the 1950s) were the big thing, aficionados became incredibly focused on the minutia of dying techniques, stitching styles, pattern cuts, brass studs and buttons. "We see information itself as a consumer item. When we do a 40-page spread on white wines, or feature pictures of every product available at the Hermes boutique in Paris, as we did recently, we know that our readers are not going to be building wine cellars or rushing off to Paris. Knowing things is an end in itself," says Saito. And manufacturers of consumer goods rely heavily on exposure in magazines like *Brutus*, *Hanako* and *Popeye*, a magazine for young men. When Levi jeans were about to introduce a new line in Japan, instead of solely relying on their ad agencies to make decisions about positioning, they met with the magazine editors, hoping to get a clue as to what the readers of these influential publications would go for.

In many ways, interests and tastes are what set Tokyo people apart and define readers. It would be useless to base a magazine entirely on class or status. Here the bank vice-president and the convenience store owner may share a common fascination with, say, vintage watches. It is just that the banker has more money to spend to satisfy his interest, while the convenience store guy only reads about it or scrimps and saves until he can afford to buy one or two. The golf enthusiast unable to afford a country club membership, which can cost millions, takes his expensive set of clubs to the local driving range, hitting balls into the void and all the while imagining glory on the links. Magazines thus become dream machines catering to the secret needs and desires of men who for the most part must live them out vicariously in their pages.

Many of the stores in Shibuya have numbers instead of names, giving the place a kind of spacy look. One of the bigger ones is simply called "0101," while another is named "109." The latter is part of the Tokyu chain, one of two that dominate this corner of the capital. *To* can also mean "ten" in Japanese and *kyu* can mean "nine," hence 109 becomes a synonym for Tokyu. Another large store is called the Seibu Seed. Needless to say, it is not a feed store. Between them, Tokyu and Seibu have about fifteen branches scattered throughout Shibuya. One of the streets emanating from Shibuya station is Tokyo's Park Avenue, *Koen Dori*, once known by the more prosaic name of Ward Office Road, which, of course, leads to the Parco department store. Parco is Italian for "park." The Seibu interests would have preferred a French word for the first department store in Tokyo dedicated to fashion, but as the French word is identical to English, it would not have had the same cachet.

Seibu's founder, Seiji Tsutsumi, has a large claim to bringing style and fashion to Tokyo. For much of the 1980s and well into the 1990s, Seibu was by far the most successful and innovative department store chain in the capital. It began in a decidedly down-market section of the city called Ikebukuro, where Seibu still has its largest store, but its natural home is in Shibuya. Seiji was the legitimate son of a property-magnate and political power broker, Yasujiro Tsutsumi. A student rebel in the 60s, when students were still rebels, and later a prize-winning novelist, he inherited probably the least promising asset of the elder Tsutsumi's vast empire of hotels and railroads. The store was then a mediocre railway terminal department store dealing mainly in daily necessities and food. It ranked at the bottom in total sales among the dozen in the capital.

Displaying a flare for marketing, Seiji moved the store to the fourth spot in five years, trailing only the mighty Mitsukoshi, Isetan and Tokyu. He immediately increased the space devoted to higher-priced consumer goods and luxury items. By 1960, he was pioneering in the sales of such unconventional items as luxury yachts and pre-fabricated homes. That year his sister, Kuniko, who had earlier moved to Europe, set up a buying office in Paris, making Seibu the first Japanese department store with an overseas office. Kuniko had established a reputation as a cultivated and fashion-conscience woman: for 25 years she reported from Paris for several Japanese fashion magazines. So, she quickly established connections with rising French designers. She introduced Yves Saint Laurent to Japan via Seibu as early as 1963. Hermes followed in 1968, and David Hechter, whom Kuniko claims to have discovered, followed later. Since then, Seibu has become virtually synonymous with European brand names and can claim to have introduced brand-conscientiousness to Japan. Seiji even picked a French word, "Saison" as the name for his holding company.

As Japan's economy began to take off in the 1960s, so did Seibu. It catered to the younger set, growing in affluence. Seiji quickly grasped the merchandising appeal of culture. His stores became entertainment centers, incorporating concert halls, cinemas and art exhibitions. In 1975 he opened the Sezon Museum of Art in his Ikebukuro store. It has mounted exhibitions of paintings by Dufy and Monet as well as numerous modern artists. At the same time, he transformed his stores into one-stop consumer service centers where the youthful clientele could buy concert tickets, life insurance or a love-boat cruise. In 1969, Seibu opened the first of its Parco stores, the first in Tokyo devoted exclusively to fashion items. Not a department store per se, it was more like a giant warehouse for boutiques. Basically, Seibu served as the landlord for dozens of small boutiques, most of which targeted their wares at women in their 20s. The opening of the huge Parco store in Shibuya set the seal on that district as THE place in Tokyo through which everything young, modern and trendy flowed into Japan. The Bubble Era years brought other, more specialized stores: "Wave," offering acres of records, tapes and compact discs; "Seed" store stocking clothes by less well knows designers; and, "Loft," a store specializing on cult memorabilia.

In the 1990s, Seibu's fortunes began to ebb. The Saison group had expanded into hotels and other enterprises less appropriate for recession years. Other department stores began to catch up and even surpassed Seibu as purveyors of style. The marketing phenomenon of the late 1990s was Tokyu Hands, especially its six-story spread in the newly developed district just south of Shinjuku Station, which helped turn that once non-descript district into a new youth shopping Mecca. It bursts with things for the handy man. One can spend hours picking through a remarkable assortment of gadgets: the Beauty Smile Trainer, a curved plastic bar that, held in the mouth, enables the user to form and keep the perfect smile; a Portable Mini Toilet for those awkward moments when traffic is heavy and you can't wait; and, a bear costume, full-sized with eyeholes, the perfect outfit for . . . well, for those times when you want to look like a bear. In 1999, Seibu was forced to close its Sezon Museum of Art, which was costing billions of yen to run. While Seibu no longer has the same cachet it once had, Seiji can still be regarded as one of the handful of people who truly transformed the look of Tokyo.

Early in the evening, the golden youth of Tokyo used to gather for evening revels at a converted warehouse in a nondescript neighborhood near the waterfront. They arrived by taxi or walked the short distance from Tamachi station. The men were all dressed sharply in double-breasted suits with wide lapels and subdued ties. A platoon of doormen stood guard to make sure that no tourists in T-shirts or Bermuda shorts were allowed inside. Spiky, colored laser lights emanated from a revolving chandelier, and as the steady thump of heavy rock music blared, the patrons jerked and swayed to the beat and waved their feathered pom poms. As the evening progressed, the tempo quickened, and the beat seemed to get stronger. "Go, Tokyo! Go!" shouted the African-American deejay from his electronic console. The dance floor was packed with people, bobbing, swaying, bobbing and swaying, all inhibitions forgotten.

Juliana's was the hottest nightclub in Tokyo. That in itself was not so remarkable. Nightclubs pass into and out of fashion as fast as hair color styles. No, something else was at work. It wasn't the colored lights, the decor or the music that drew customers every night by the thousands. It was the otachi-dai, or the platform at the far end of the dance floor, raised high enough so that the dancers below could gaze up at the spectacle of office ladies performing like show girls. They arrived wearing conventional clothes, but once they passed through the airlock-type entrance, a transformation took place. Inside, they headed straight for the ladies room, where they shed their street clothes, stuffing them into lockers conveniently provided by the management. Then they squeezed into glittering, white, orange or black mini-skirts. Now, dripping with sequins, their shoulders bared and their midrifts naked, they totter on tall spiked heels to the stage.

A palpable feeling of sexuality permeated. Yet, strangely, there didn't seem to be much action going on. Juliana's was never a boys-meet-girls kind of place. For all their suggestive clothing, the young women were not looking to be picked up. Mostly, they danced by themselves, seemingly lost in their own private narcissism. On the dance floor below, the men danced alone, too, facing the stage so that they could watch the women above. As the witching hour of midnight approached, most of the women left the stage and returned to the ladies room to change back into their ordinary street clothes for the taxi or, more likely, the long commuter train ride back home alone. After all, the next morning was another working day.

One day about three years after it opened, the police visited Juliana's management. Some residents had complained that young women were using the outdoor fire escapes and foyers of nearby apartments to change into dancing togs. Others grumbled that by running a "strip show," Juliana's was degrading the neighborhood. The authorities demanded that the platform be removed and a stricter dress code enforced. The disco duly complied and replaced the platform with a smaller one where only professional dancers would perform. Nevertheless, patronage fell of dramatically, and before losses grew too large, the management decided to close to preserve, as one put it, Juliana's "honorable name." Thus, the disco which gave the Japanese language a new word, *bodicon* for 'body-conscious' and for 'tight-fitting dress', went back to being a warehouse.

Juliana's opened a year after Japan's financial collapse but before the resulting recession ushered in a new feeling of sobriety. In a way, it was one final burst of pyrotechnics of the Bubble Era. Clearly, it also signified a kind of sexual liberation, yet one of a strange kind. The strict social and moral codes that had once channelled women into early marriage and motherhood were breaking down. Yet, there were relatively few real careers open to them, even during the resulting labor shortage in the male-dominated economy. So, failing to win respect for the knowledge and skills that they brought to the workplace, women used the only asset they had left, their bodies. Or, that's what many social critics and pop psychologists opined. The girls themselves had another way of putting it. Said one, "I just love to see those men gather to watch me dance."

Other signposts of changing morals could be found around Tokyo. Anyone who scanned the news stands at railroad kiosks and bookstores might notice that a lot of otherwise respectable publications were loudly touting their "hair-nude" pictures inside. Although erotic woodblock prints were common during Edo times, Japanese have in modern times been rather straight-laced about pornography. Anti-obscenity laws prohibited photographs of women showing pubic hair, and censors faithfully blotted them out in foreign publications like *Playboy* or *Penthouse*. No such strictures applied to *manga*, or comic books, which are often crudely pornographic. The Tokyo Metropolitan Government once examined more than a thousand manga and found that fully half the plots revolved around sex. Inside, 96 percent of females depicted were between 13 and 29, one third were drawn with bare breasts and 17 percent were fully naked. You see men reading these books openly and unashamedly on commuter trains and other public places everywhere in Tokyo. Then, a young actress named Rei Miyazawa published a book of nude photographs about herself that bared everything; she loudly proclaimed that she had nothing to be ashamed of. The editors of the popular women's magazine *An-An* smelled a trend, and asked its readers if they would like to have their own nude photos taken by Kishin Shinoyama, the photographer who had snapped Miyazawa, and published in the magazine. To their astonishment, some 1,626 women applied, most of them ordinary office ladies or college students with no special aspirations to becoming film stars or celebrities.

Soon it seemed that every weekly magazine, even those dealing with ordinary topics of the day like politics or money scandals, were running at least some fully nude pictures of young women and loudly proclaiming their contents in banner headlines on the cover. Again, as with the night club Juliana's, the girls were not necessarily professional models, and in many cases were not even paid for posing. It was like they were making some kind of statement. The girls did not always strike provocative poses or stand in voluptuous settings. Often enough, they were simply pictured standing unsmilingly naked amid the clutter of their own tiny apartments. Clearly a social revolution of some kind was taking place among Japan's young women, but it was a half-formed revolution.

Italian fashion photographer Olivielo Toscani came to Tokyo on assignment for Bennetton, whose arresting images have created controversy around the world. Based on what he had observed on Milan — Japanese descending on designer shops and buying up anything with a famous label regardless of the design, he planned to shoot photos around the theme of "fashion victim." He expected to document what he imagined was the unthinking Japanese devotion to chic brands. After exploring the Harajuku and Shibuya districts, however, he saw that his plan needed reassessing. The expected victims sporting Prada sandals, Louis Vuitton bags and Chanel suits were there all right, but so were the young people whose looks, to Toscani's eye, fairly screamed creativity and individuality. The odd combinations of colors, a gauze blouse over a T-shirt three sizes too small, the purple hair and pierced eyebrows made him re-think Tokyo style. "These kids don't care if they are laughed at, they're not showing off. They seem to be creating not just a new fashion but a new culture," he mused.

Creative? Yes. Individual? Maybe. Superficial? Definitely. It is difficult to call it individuality when all the individuals in a group behave the same way. Fashion in Tokyo is a statement of personality, tastes and even interests — maybe more so than anywhere else in the world. In Tokyo, fashion is a definer, a badge or uniform, informing others of who the wearer is and where he or she fits into the scheme of things. Fashion functions in the same way as business cards, physically assigning roles and categories. Reggae and hip hop fans wear baggy pants, oversize training outfits and large woolen caps no matter what the season. Neo-hippies wear long flowered skirts, weave fake braids into their hair and have three or four pierced earrings in each ear. Tokyo abounds with Goths, punks, low riders, and even followers of 1960s British beat fashion who ride Vespas and wear skinny suits.

Tokyo is a place where anything goes, but that anything must be done right. There is no half way. Fashion is intense, but it can be short-lived. Fashion and playfulness are for the young and unmarried. That is why parents are rarely concerned when their daughter leaves the house for a Sunday afternoon stroll dressed like what any other parent in any other big city would call a "working girl." Parents are tolerant. They can be certain that she will be at the office in conservative attire the next morning. And just as soon as a girl gets married she will disappear into the doughty fashion wasteland of the wife and mother. As soon as a boy starts working after college graduation, he will set aside the dog collar, and that hole in his earlobe will close up from lack of use. But in the meantime, anything goes.

© Cecilia Lim

## A State of Mind

Technically, Harajuku does not exist as a place. The area stretching along Omote-sando Avenue from Aoyama-dori to the Meiji Shrine is identified on maps as Jingumae. There is a Harajuku Station on the Yamanote line, with its attractive Tudor-style facade, but the real Harajuku district is a state-of-mind. It instantly conjures images of youth, fashion and a kind of tame rebellion associated with outlandish clothes and hair styles. As one writer has put it, "Harajuku has a mood, up beat, an age, young, and a price, expensive." The area began to move to a youthful beat in the late 1960s, just after the Olympic Games. Many young people were attracted to the neighborhood's American ambiance that had been established by the Washington Heights military dependent's quarters where Yoyogi Park is now. The apartments were torn down in 1964 to create the Olympic Village, and those quarters were demolished to make the park. At about that time, young people were beginning to accumulate a little spending money to buy far-out garments being sold in stores along Omote-sando and along a parallel street, Takeshita-dori. The habitués eventually acquired a name, *Harajuku-zoku*, or the Harajuku tribe.

Omote-sando is one of the few avenues in the capital that has the feeling of a European-style grand boulevard. Indeed, the organization of businesses along the route calls itself the Harajuku Champs Elysee Association. The street, which in Japanese means "pathway leading to the holy shrine" was laid out shortly after the death of the Emperor Meiji when a large memorial shrine was built at one end on land that was once owned by a nobleman. The road was extended to Aoyama-dori, where at the time, a streetcar line ran. At one time, it was lined mainly with merchants selling religious charms, not to mention umbrellas and other practical things for the pilgrims from all over the country who came to see the famous shrine. The memorial still exists today, of course, and on New Year's Day people by the tens of thousands stream up the boulevard to visit and pray. But on any other day the street life along the boulevard has a completely different ambience.

On Sunday, the boulevard is thronged with Tokyo's color kids, their hair, shoes and clothes dyed a rainbow of bright colors, gawking at the boutiques that line the route and gawking at themselves. Some of the stores go back a long time. Kiddy Land, now a huge toy emporium, got its start selling kitchenware to the families of American occupation forces. The venerable Oriental Bazaar still has the feeling of a place where one goes to buy something for the folks back in Iowa. Many of the other stores affect a continental tone. It seems like more French is spoken here than Japanese. One passes by dozens of Galeries de Pop, or Chats Noir, or Cafes de Rope. La Foret department store is the place where the kyogaru goes to get outfitted. It is full of ultra-chic little boutiques with nonsense names like "Here There," "Clutch," "Milk Bay" (clothes, not dairy products), "Xi" and the "Nice Claup" (originally Nice Clap until someone pointed out that it referred to a social disease.)

Pretty soon, one notices the absence of pachinko parlors, "Hostess Clubs," and love hotels. The authorities banned these forms of adult entertainment, not to mention noisy factories, crematoriums and brothels, because of the presence of the sacred Meiji Shrine nearby. It gives the neighborhood an innocent ambiance. Even the condom shop looks like a candy store. On a busy street corner, where one would expect to find, say, a Baskin-Robbins ice cream store, stands "Condomania." Inside are 100 flavors of condoms — textured, scented, colored, even ones that glow-in-the-dark: "Beach Boys" (large), "Michiko London," and "Rubber Yum." Some come in bright, striped boxes archly labeled "Life Savers." Takeshita-dori is given over entirely to the teen-age set. The stores have names like "Funky Gang," and sell stone-washed jeans and pullover shirts. Girls in school uniforms amble down the alley eating crepes and jalapeno-flavored popcorn, shopping for pictures of their favorite television and movie stars at the "idol shops."

On the right side of Omote-sando stands a line of brown concrete apartment buildings. Many of them now rent space to boutiques and antique shops, like the other buildings along the avenue. But they bear a closer look. These buildings were the very first Western-style apartment buildings in Tokyo. The Dojunkai (Mutual Profits Association) was a quasi-government housing corporation that was set up after the Great Kanto Earthquake in 1923 to build new homes for the thousands who had been made homeless in the conflagration. Traditionally, the only kind of multi-family housing units in the capital were the *nagaya*, long, one-story wooden row houses. The Dojunkai were made out of concrete instead (which is why they survived American fire-bombing in 1945) and were several stories in height. They still retained many Japanese features, however. The interiors were designed with tatami mat measurements in mind and small vestibules in the front of the apartments allow the occupant to remove his shoes before entering.

Some apartment buildings were erected in the shitamachi that was devastated by the quake, but many others, including those along Omote-sando, were built specifically for the emerging salaryman class living in the hills to the west. The movement of people to this part of town had been accelerated by the devastation wrought by the quake. When the apartments were first put on the market, newspapers reported about several features they thought were novel: shelves in the kitchen, wheeled bins for storing coal in the winter or rice that could be pulled out from under the counter, and private toilets with Western-style plumbing. A central courtyard with trees and a playground also figured in the design. But at 37 meters square, they are small, even by current cramped standards. Since the Dojunkai organization was disbanded in the 1960s not much was done to preserve these buildings. About half of the originals have been torn down, most recently the graceful complex in Daikanyama, where the late Kiyoshi Atsumi (famous for starring in Tora-san movies) had a getaway apartment. Today, the buildings exude a pleasant weathered look, especially when the rough brown exteriors are set against the russet colored leaves on the zelkova trees along Omote-sando in late autumn.

— T.C.

# 6

# Outsiders

Since that day not all that long ago in 1853 when four uninvited American navy ships arrived in Tokyo Bay bringing an end to 250 years of Japanese isolation, *gaijin*, or foreigners, in Tokyo have been a curiosity, regarded with a mixture of respect, amusement and disdain. Although in many respects, Tokyo is a world-class international city, the prevailing attitude towards foreigners remains provincial. To be sure, the days when department store clerks would scatter in fear at the sight of an approaching foreign customer — even if that customer spoke fluent Japanese — are gone, but they are not distant. As recently as the early 1980s, non-Asian-appearing foreigners in Tokyo were greeted with stares from fellow subway riders and shouts of "herro!" from drunken businessmen on train platforms at night.

Although the number of registered foreigners in Tokyo has been steadily increasing, they are still relatively few. Out of Tokyo's daytime population of 11 million only 274,000 or 1.9 percent are foreigners. Americans are still the largest group among Westerners in Tokyo. The community was 13,600 strong at the end of 1998, more than twice the number of British citizens, the next largest group. It is this continued American influence that sets Tokyo apart from many other Asian capitals where the Western influence is clearly and for obvious historical reasons decidedly European. In Tokyo, there are no pukkah fans like those in the Long Bar at Raffles in Singapore. No one takes high tea at the Okura Hotel as they do at The Peninsula in Hong Kong. And it is still difficult to find baguettes or café au lait for breakfast as authentic as that served in Saigon. Rather than inheriting the graceful trappings of the colonial European life still evident in Kuala Lumpur, Tokyo's West is the West of the boisterous and exuberant post-World War II American GI. The pop culture energy takes its cues from the young carefree Americans who descended on the city after the war, just when Tokyo was remaking itself once again, having been bombed into oblivion by those same Americans just a few years before.

The occupation forces are long gone. Though contingents of American troops remain in the Tokyo area, they are largely invisible. They never appear in the city in uniform, never ride in jeep convoys through the main streets. But the American tinge to the modern city that is Tokyo is unmistakable. Just as Japanese electronics makers took ideas from the West and improved upon them, the neon-blazing entertainment districts like Kabukicho, Ginza and Shibuya are blinding examples of Times Square and The Strip in Las Vegas taken to their wildest conclusion. Even the details are telling: the English spelling is American — no "centres" here — elevators are not lifts, and when you enter a building you are on the first floor, not the ground floor. The only disorienting detail is that traffic moves on the left, as in Britain, a habit instituted in the Meiji Reformation days of the late 1800s, when all that was modern was British.

Old Tokyo hands — you have to have lived in Tokyo in the 1950s to qualify — still fondly remember the days when Americans ruled. "When I first got here after the Korean War, I was still a GI, 24 years old. When I used to walk down the streets — I was making newsreels and we were allowed to wear civilian clothes — the Japanese would get off to one side of the road and bow deeply. Whether it was fear or respect or annoyance, you couldn't tell because all you could see were the tops of their heads," recalls Corky Alexander, 70, publisher of *The Tokyo Weekender*, the bi-weekly chronicle of Tokyo's expat society. "Back then, America was idealized and idolized. In those days, when you were asked where you were from and your answer was America, the reaction was one of awe and respect. You were treated as if you had just achieved some major accomplishment. It was very flattering. We would go to bars and all the hostesses would tell us what movie stars we looked like. I was either Donald O'Connor or Robert Mitchum," he remembers, a wistful smile crossing his face.

In the early post-war days, young Americans were flush with cash and eager to take advantage of the money-making possibilities. "Everybody was wheeling and dealing. It was a carpetbagger atmosphere. Guys were buying up land, opening shops and making piles of money. But it changed, and my theory is that it was the Tokyo Olympics in 1964 that sparked the change." The Olympics worked beautifully. The Games went off without a hitch. The success of the Games gave Japan back its pride and the whole country was on fire with enthusiasm. "In fact, some might say they got their self-confidence back to the point of arrogance. It built and built until the Bubble burst," Corky says. The bursting of the Bubble had a leveling effect, and attitudes towards Americans have grown more complex. There is still respect but also resentment as Tokyo looks for a way toward "normalcy" in the relationship.

Just as Japanese attitudes towards Americans have changed, the American expat community in Tokyo itself has changed. "Nowadays, there's no feeling of camaraderie like there was once," Corky laments. "In the old days, all the expats sent here were company presidents — the average age was probably 60 or so — and the atmosphere was different. Nowadays, since the financial hotshots have taken over, you get the brokers making a million dollars, speaking fluent Japanese — I hate 'em — and their young families. These days, the biggest issue at the American Club is 'where can I breast feed and can we change diapers in the lounge?'"

The Tokyo American Club, a sprawling compound, occupies expensive acreage right in the heart of Minato Ward, expat central, the part of the city with the largest concentration of Americans. Founded in 1928 and operating under the principle that "Everybody needs friends. Everybody needs a place where they feel like they belong," the club offers a refuge for its 3,700 members. Facilities include five restaurants, two bars, a beauty salon, a bookstore, a fitness center, pool and a 4,000-title video collection. Classes are offered in everything from pre-natal yoga to taiko drumming, from salsa dancing to karate. All this comes with a price, of course. Membership costs on average $15,000 for the joining fee plus about $200 a month per family.

Michael and Karen Kaye[*] are two of the new breed of expats, the type that old-timers like Corky find so unexciting. They, along with their two children, Gabby*, 8, and Matt*, 5, moved to Tokyo from a New York suburb in 1998 when Michael, a head of procurement for a major U.S. multi-national, was transferred to Tokyo, the company's headquarters in Asia. Karen had spent a year in Tokyo as a university exchange student so was familiar with the city, the life and the language. Their move to Tokyo was facilitated by the use of a relocation company that handled all the moving details and continues to provide services. The company helped to find their apartment, served as a go-between with the building management, and even took Karen on a familiarization tour of the local supermarket to point out sugarless yogurt and low-fat milk, bits of information that would have held little interest for Corky's expats of yesteryear.

The Kayes chose to live in the Azabu district of Minato. One of the last of the central districts of Tokyo to be developed — an early 1900s guide to the city nicknamed Azabu "voice of the insects" — it soon became the home of embassies and high ranking foreign business executives. Rents for spacious apartments in the area can go as high as $15,000 a month, although it takes a trained eye to realize that this is such an expensive neighborhood. To the casual observer, Azabu looks much like any other residential district of Tokyo. Large single-family homes are mixed in with rundown two-story apartment buildings and newer condominiums. Few buildings have lawns or gardens of any significant size, and most have no driveways or garages. A closer look, however reveals the details that say this is an upscale area catering to the affluent outsider: an abundance of antique shops, stores selling traditional Japanese craft items, gourmet shops and clothing stores boasting an unusually wide range of sizes.

The Kayes' building, a five-story apartment complex with a rare circular driveway setting it off from the street, is occupied entirely by fellow foreigners on expense accounts. Their unit, with four bedrooms and three baths, goes for about $8,500 per month. It makes no concessions to life in Japan. There are no rooms with tatami mats. There is no entrance hall for removing shoes. On the contrary, it is equipped with appliances like a built-in oven and a dishwasher that even the most affluent of upper middle class Japanese would be unlikely to have seen in a home before.

Michael's job keeps him travelling most of the time visiting suppliers and customers all over Asia. His biggest concern is the time it takes to get to and from the inconveniently located Narita airport. While he's interested in getting to know Tokyo, he has little free time on his hands. His time is taken up commuting to his office in suburban Hino — an hour and a half each way — and making the two-hour trek out to the airport for his frequent business trips. Karen's life, on the other hand, since the moment she arrived has been a whirlwind of social activity centered around the kids' school, the American Club and friends she made through these places. Weekly parties, lectures on Japan, walking tours of old Tokyo and Japanese language classes fill the days. Shuttling the kids to school, to play dates with friends and to various after school lessons also takes time. In fact, expat spouses who move to Tokyo from Singapore or Hong Kong often complain about the lifestyle: Tokyo does not have the legion of domestic helpers that are so readily available in those cities.

Of course, not all Americans in Tokyo are executives and company managers. Americans in Tokyo also work as middle managers in advertising firms, as public relations people for manufacturers, and, of course, as English teachers. But these are local hires, Americans who came to Japan and were hired in country and without the very generous compensation packages their compatriots transferred from abroad receive. These days some level of competency in Japanese language is required for a position in business. And those wishing to teach English need some sort of qualification, if only a bachelor's degree. Until about the mid-80s, any native speaker of English, provided he or she conformed to the stereotype image of a native speaker, i.e. not of Asian descent, could waltz into town, pick up a teaching job and quickly be earning $100 an hour.

Americans and other Westerners who are interested in making money and getting to know modern Japan choose Tokyo. Those seeking enlightenment or schooling in Japanese arts head for Kyoto. It is in the ancient capital where one finds the Canadian master of the tea ceremony, the American studying *raku* pottery techniques and the German practicing Zen meditation. Tokyo is inevitably disappointing for the Westerner in search of the "real" Japan. Other gaijin have integrated into Japanese life with varying degrees of success. Finnish-born Marutei Tsurunen gained fame when he became the first Caucasian-Japanese ever elected to a town council, in Yugawara near Tokyo. He made two respectable albeit unsuccessful bids to become the first Caucasian in the House of Councilors, the Diet's upper chamber.

Perhaps the most famous ex-American in Tokyo is the former sumo wrestling star from Hawaii who goes by the name Konishiki. In the early 1990s, Konishiki's quest to become the first gaijin to achieve the rank of *yokozuna*, or grand champion, riveted the country. He had won the requisite number of matches, but doubts lingered whether he, or any other foreign wrestler, had that undefinable quality of athletic dignity that the Japanese call *hinkaku*. Konishiki did not help his chances either by complaining in *The New York Times* that he was being denied yokozuna status because he was a foreigner. It fell to another Hawaiian, Akebono (nee Chad Rowen) to become the first foreign-born yokozuna in early 1993 after a smashing victory in a New Year's tournament. Konishiki has since retired from the ring and became a television pitchman.

If the Americans are the most visible foreigners in Tokyo, it is the Koreans who are the most invisible. The total of 274,000 foreigners in Tokyo is deceptive. It includes 94,650 ethnic Korean residents, the vast majority of whom were born and raised in

Japan. The case of the Koreans in Japan is a sensitive subject, not one that is raised casually or in social conversation. Their history in Japan is linked to Japan's annexation of Korea in 1910. Japan confiscated land from Koreans, exported the rice crop to Japan and in general caused severe economic hardship. Many Koreans, considered Imperial subjects of Japan, migrated to the country in search of work. They were met with discrimination and hardship. Thousands were murdered by crazed Japanese in the aftermath of the Great Kanto Earthquake in 1923. But by 1938, there were about 800,000 Korean laborers who had come to Japan to try to earn a living. During the war years, more Koreans were forcibly brought to Japan to work and estimates have it that at the end of the war there were more than two million Koreans living in the country. At that time, many Koreans, particularly those forced to migrate during the war years, elected to return to Korea, but large numbers of those who had arrived before the war stayed. Having left Korea when their land was confiscated and their livelihood taken away, they had nothing to return to. Since the end of the war, the resident Korean population in Japan as a whole has remained a fairly constant 600,000.

During Japan's colonial occupation of Korea, Koreans in Japan were considered Japanese citizens but with the end of the war and the end of colonization, Koreans were again classified as aliens and to this day are required to register as such. This means that in Tokyo there are about 94,000 people, over 600,000 nationwide, who are classified as foreigners but have never known any country other than Japan. The majority of these people use Japanese names, speak no Korean and are virtually indistinguishable by outward appearance from their Japanese neighbors. But the consequences of being classified as aliens, even as permanent residents, are real. As non-Japanese, they may not work as civil servants or as regular public school teachers and they may encounter difficulties in choosing a marriage partner, establishing a business or renting a home. Barred from many professions, some Koreans went into businesses on the shady, if not illegal, side by running pachinko parlors, loan companies and other gambling related businesses. Some became involved in organized crime. These negative images and stereotypes of Koreans persist in Japan and along with them Japanese prejudice against resident Koreans.

This discrimination has taken its toll. A criminal gang called the Dragons, based in the Ikebukuro section of Tokyo, has been making its presence known over the past few years. The gang, led by disaffected Korean youths, is comprised largely of Koreans and equally disaffected Chinese and Vietnamese young men. The gang seems intent on committing violent crimes, and their disregard for the traditional Japanese gang system of honor and duty has scared even the local yakuza away, or so the local media, never loathe to sensationalizing any story related to gaijin and crime, has portrayed them.

Much of the increase in the crime rate — still low by international standards — in Japan in the last ten years is popularly attributed to the increase in the number of foreigners. Indeed when a robbery or random-seeming murder is committed, it is not unusual for initial reports in the media to include the information that foreigners are suspected as the perpetrators, reflecting a sort of round-up-the-usual-suspect mentality. A cursory look at the statistics does suggest that a disproportionate number of crimes nationwide are committed by foreigners. In 1997, foreigners accounted for 2 percent of the arrests, but only 1 percent of the population. But these numbers are misleading. Of the 9,850 foreigners picked up by police that year, 7,123, or almost two-thirds of the total, were charged with immigration-related offences.

In Tokyo, the largest concentration of gaijin can be found in Shinjuku Ward, and the largest concentration within Shinjuku can be found in Hyakunincho, just north of the Kabukicho entertainment district. Hyakunincho, literally "Hundred Man Town," was named for the Hundred-Man Militia, the low-level rifle-carrying samurai who were loyal to Lord Kiyonari Naito during the Edo Period. They camped close to the Naito estate in the area now Shinjuku Gyoen Park. The neighborhood is now home to Tokyo's more recently arrived Korean, Chinese, Thai and other Southeast Asian people. Along Okubo Street, the area's main drag, between Okubo Station and Meiji Street, conversations in Korean, Chinese or Thai far outnumber those in Japanese. In the 600-meter stretch of the street, there are more than 20 Korean barbecue restaurants, an almost equal number of Chinese restaurants and many shops with signs written only in Hangul or Thai. During the local business association's sales promotions, announcements on the shopping street's speaker system are broadcast in Mandarin, Korean, English and, then almost as an after thought, in Japanese.

To many Tokyo residents, the mention of the name of the district still strikes fear in their hearts. It is not because of the long-gone militia, but because Hyakunincho has the reputation, due to its concentration of Asian foreigners, as a bastion of crime and sleaze. In addition to the restaurants, language schools and grocery stores selling Thai fish sauce and kimchee, there is an abundance of pachinko parlors, Korean and Chinese "esthetic salons" or massage parlors, and love hotels. The love hotels, lining the narrow lanes between Kabukicho and Okubo Street, can easily be distinguished from normal small hotels: the entrances are hidden behind high walls, their rates (guests can choose a two-hour "rest" or an overnight "stay".) are posted outside and many of them display signs saying, "Prohibit [sic] to go into with foreign ladies who are waiting on the road." This is a reference to the Russian hookers who ply their trade in Hyakunincho each night.

"Yes, there are hookers here and, yes, there's an underworld element. But I find the neighborhood interesting. There's no question that it has changed though — and changed several times. Until about the mid-80s, this was just another typical Tokyo neighborhood. During the Bubble Years though, when so many foreign workers came to Japan, Kabukicho, the traditional place for them, wasn't big enough to hold them. So, Hyakunincho, the next neighborhood up, took on the overflow," says Fumio Takahashi, a businessman who has worked at his company's Hyakunincho office for 20 years. "But it used to be worse," he continues, "about three years ago. The police decided to crack down on the more obvious violators, and now people are more discreet. There are yakuza operating here, collecting fees from the hookers. But they," he says, making the Japanese gesture for gangster, an index finger running down the cheek to indicate a scar, as he looks around furtively to make sure none of "them" are around to see, "keep to their own business and won't bother anyone who's not involved." In fact, they rarely ask for protection money from the neighbourhood shops. Instead, they politely come by regularly "selling" bouquets of plastic flowers, restaurant decorations or umbrella stands at prices too good for the proprietors to refuse.

"Anyway, I like it here because I feel like I'm not in Japan. There are plenty of interesting people to meet and talk to and certainly a lot of good food," he observes from his regular seat in Chuka Hanten,* a Chinese restaurant in the area. Chuka Hanten is one of the few Chinese restaurants in Hyakunincho that looks like it is going after Japanese customers — the signs outside describing the food as "authentic, cheap and delicious" are written in Japanese. Inside the small room with ten tables is festively decorated in bright red with lanterns, and posters of China, looking just what a Chinese restaurant is supposed to look like to a Japanese customer. Yuriko Honma,* the owner of the restaurant, came to Japan from Fujian Province in China three years ago with her Japanese husband and now uses a Japanese name. For Yuriko, one of the 68,000 Chinese in Tokyo, life in Japan is more difficult than she expected it to be. "When I first came, I really liked Tokyo. It was so clean and everyone seemed so nice. But now I don't feel that way. To a Chinese person, it feels small, cramped. Here in Tokyo, if you don't work you can't live. In China, if you work and save a little you can have a pretty good life, but here rents are expensive. You have to pay for the kids' schooling. Everything costs a lot."

Still, Chen Dan,* chef and waiter at the restaurant, says he's in Tokyo for the money. He lives in a tiny 6 square meter apartment with no bath or kitchen, about the size of his bathroom back home in Fujian. His rent is about $200. But he was prepared for the life here. A network of friends and relatives returning from stints working in Tokyo had told him exactly what to expect. "My plan is to stay until I'm 30, five more years. By then, I'll have saved enough to open my own restaurant at home." Chen spends all his time working, feeling no compulsion to get to know Tokyo or Japan. "I'm not really interested in Japanese culture. It all comes from China anyway. I feel that people here don't like me, but to be frank, if you ask any Chinese person here or in China, he will say he doesn't like Japanese. That's how we were raised. That's what we were taught in school," Chen explains unapologetically.

"I know that we are among the lucky ones to have jobs now that the economy is so bad. There are so many people overstaying their visas trying to make a living, but no matter how hard they intend to work, they can't find jobs that pay enough to make it worthwhile. That's what a lot of people who come into the restaurant tell me — Malaysians, Chinese, Filipinos — that its tough to find a job now," says Yuriko.

David Sedo* can attest to that. Most nights, David can be found on the streets of the Roppongi district handing out flyers for Tokyo's self-proclaimed "No.1 disco," featuring "cheap drinks, hip-hop, R&B, soul, reggae and a 'Boom-Boom-Boom Show'." This is far from his home in Ghana and a far cry from what he would like to be doing. It is a temporary job, paying about $6 an hour, a stop gap until he finds his next construction gig and can get back to making some real money. After so many years in Japan, he thought he would be doing much better by now. David, now in his mid-40s, came to Japan to seek his fortune. He left his native land in 1986 to work as a construction engineer in Libya. After five years there, having grown tired of the discrimination he says he felt there as a sub-Saharan, non-Muslim African, and not yet ready to return to Ghana, he began to look elsewhere for opportunity. "America was my first choice, but I was told it would take something like five years just to get a tourist visa. Of course, I couldn't apply from Libya. They told me to go back to Ghana, get a job, establish myself and after a few years maybe I could get a tourist visa. Well, I didn't have five years and I couldn't establish myself in Ghana — that's why I wanted to leave in the first place. So I went to the Japanese Embassy applied for a tourist visa and got it in no time. They were so naive," he laughs heartily.

For the first three months of his stay in Tokyo, David was one of the approximately 1,500 Ghanaians legally in Japan. Then he joined the ranks of the "overstayers" or "overs," as they refer to themselves. The most recent estimate of their numbers is 271,048, a number that has been steadily declining since the high of 298,646 in 1993. At the peak of the Bubble Era, "overs" were not just tolerated, they were recognized as a necessity. After all, who else would want the jobs commonly known as the 3Ks — *kiken, kitanai, kitsui,* or dangerous, dirty and difficult. They worked largely in construction and the contractors were glad to have them.

David arrived in Japan in 1991 with no contacts, no relatives and no network of friends to offer support. But he quickly learned the ropes and found a construction job with the help of one of the many "agencies," run largely by fellow overs from Bangladesh and Iran, specializing in placing the illegal workers with construction contractors. David paid the agent an up-front fee of $830 per placement. "They probably get a fee from the employer too. And if for some reason the job didn't work out and you need another placement you have to pay another $830. I paid the fee three times before I found a job that lasted for a while." Since 1991 David has had several jobs, the longest one lasting just over four years. "I made enough to save quite a bit. Especially since I was living in a company dormitory and most of my meals were included."

His status as an overstayer was never a source of concern. "Being illegal is no big deal. If you keep out of trouble, the police aren't going to bother you. I've been stopped several times by the police but they never ask for my ID card and I've never been close to being deported." His illegal status hasn't interfered with workers' benefits either. After sustaining an on-the-job injury, the doctor's bills were covered by the national health insurance. Then his employer tried to dock his pay for the time spent recovering. Since it was a work-related injury the labor ministry went to bat for him and ordered his boss to pay up. "Even though we are working illegally, these government institutions help us. They have no connection at all with the immigration or police records. I was never afraid that I would be reported."

In late 1998, the effect of the prolonged recession finally trickled down to David, and he was laid off. He had to move out of company housing and spend much of the money he had saved on an apartment. His room, in a two-story apartment building about 15 minutes from Shinjuku Station by express train, is about 15 sq m and costs him about $300 a month. While he looks for a new job, he works part-time in Roppongi handing out flyers for the disco. "I don't like the work at all. The club tries to project a black image and certain types of Japanese girls go there looking to meet black men. Some nights if there aren't enough black men, just whites or Asians, they complain," he says.

"I haven't felt racial discrimination, but most of us Africans here in Japan have learned that when Japanese people ask us where we are from, not to answer "Africa" or the name of our country. I used to answer truthfully and the reaction was always the same: "Oh, Africa" in a bored voice and then the person would walk away. But if I answer "America" or "Canada" or "the Caribbean," they are very interested in learning all about me. So there's a kind of snobbery, not exactly racist but they don't seem to want to mingle with people from less developed countries."

Tokyo's relationship with gaijin is still an odd mixture of condescension and sensitivity, revealing the fact that the society has not yet come to terms with the concept of the "other." Politicians still regularly make rude public remarks referring to different nationality groups — saying things like minorities in America are the cause of crime and low productivity — only to be forced into an apology the very next day. Until the mid-1980s, massage parlors providing extra services were commonly called Turkish Baths. When the Turkish Embassy protested that the terminology was insulting, the Turkish Baths suddenly became Soaplands. Ironically, in the late 90s, these same businesses started to call themselves Korean Esthetic Salons, leading one to wonder how long it will take before the Korean Embassy lodges its complaint.

Even Corky Alexander, the old Tokyo hand, admits that he is still mystified by the way Japanese see themselves in relation to others. "Even though they may know I've been here for 45 years, they still ask if I can eat Japanese food, whether I can use chopsticks and compliment me profusely when I produce a simple Japanese greeting like *konnichiwa*. I'm still trying to figure out what part of the Japanese psyche it is that makes them feel that they are so mysterious and so different that no one else could possibly speak their language or eat their food."

Foreigners in Tokyo are especially exotic and fascinating when they talk about Japan, where self-examination prompted by a foreigner's view has been a national obsession since the days of Lafcadio Hearn, an early observer of the country and culture. Every Wednesday night at 10:00, thousands of Japanese across the country tune into Tokyo Broadcasting Systems popular "Strange Japanese Habits," a TV talk show featuring a panel of 50 long-term foreign residents complaining about Japan in fluent Japanese. The 50, representing almost as many countries, face off with the film director and comedian Takeshi Kitano, retired sumo star Konishiki, and a few other Japanese celebrities to complain about anything from the local education system to the Japanese penchant for toilet humor.

They shout, they stomp, they argue with one another, often making the descent into name calling, and rarely rising above the intellectual level of the average eight-year-old. This particular show is only the most recent incarnation in a long line of TV entertainment featuring gaijin either making fools of themselves or displaying how, despite incalculable odds, they have somehow been able to master some aspect of Japan's unique culture.

The show's Japanese name, *Koko ga hen, Nippon*, literally means 'Hey Japan, Here's Where You're Strange'. The title is a play on the old epithet, *henna gaijin,* or strange foreigner. The show almost always features gaijin who speak fluent Japanese and, thus, are considered strange. The show works on several levels at once: it provides an amusing showcase for several varieties of henna gaijin; it begins a cross cultural dialogue of sorts; and above all, it offers a forum for that beloved Japanese past time, navel-gazing.

In one classic episode, a group of Japanese high school girls appeared on the show in conjunction with the evening's theme: Japanese youth. The particular girls selected for the show were obviously not of the more studious variety. They were representatives of the trend-setting *kogyaru* type, with dyed hair, currently fashionable loose socks that look like leg warmers and very short skirts. Many of the foreigners yelled that they were "the shame of Japan" and that if these girls represented the future, "I fear for Japan." The girls were defiant and offered as their defense: "This is Japan. This is the way we do things." The Japanese panel of celebrities seized the opportunity and joined with the foreigners in pleading with the girls to think more seriously about their futures.

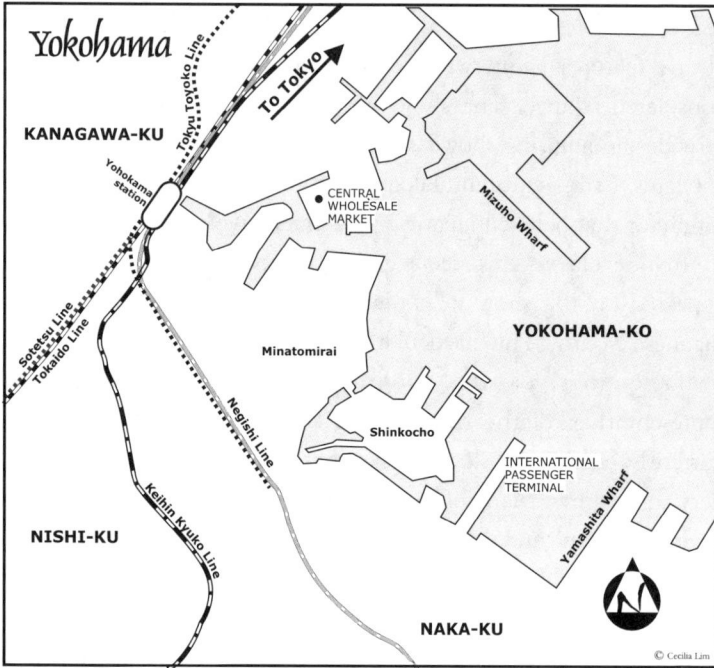

Yokohama

KANAGAWA-KU

Tokyu Toyoko Line

To Tokyo

Yokohama station

Sotetsu Line

Tokaido Line

CENTRAL WHOLESALE MARKET

Mizuho Wharf

Minatomirai

Negishi Line

Shinkocho

YOKOHAMA-KO

INTERNATIONAL PASSENGER TERMINAL

Yamashita Wharf

Keihin Kyuko Line

NISHI-KU

NAKA-KU

© Cecilia Lim

## New Life in the Old Port

The engines thumped, children pulled on the throttles and clambered up and down the ladders. But the venerable passenger liner *Hikawa Maru* is not going anywhere. It is permanently berthed on the waterfront of Yokohama. The atmosphere on board reeks of the 1920s and 1930s, the grand age of steamer lines, when the wealthy crossed the Pacific Ocean in style. One can imagine how passengers must have whiled away the long hours of passage sitting in richly brocaded easy chairs and reading or playing mahjong with other passengers. An old travel poster reminds one that in the years before the war the old vessel regularly plied the waters between Seattle and Yokohama. "It's everyone's dream to sail on the *Hikawa Maru*," declares James Cagney in the 1945 movie melodrama, **Blood on the Sun**.

For years, many gaijin first experienced Japan by looking through the porthole or leaning over the railing as the *Hikawa Maru* or some other liner slowly maneuvered along side the quay. Moments after setting foot on land, the traveler was immersed in strange new sights and sounds. Lafcadio Hearn remembered his first day in Japan that way after disembarking. "'T'is at first a delightfully odd confusion as you look down through the interminable flutter of flags and swaying dark blue drapery, all made beautiful and mysterious with Japanese or Chinese lettering. Each building seems to have a fantastic prettiness of its own. Nothing is exactly like anything else, and all is bewilderingly novel."

Not being a medieval city or a temple town, Yokohama was something of a blank slate, waiting for somebody to write on it. And Europeans did most of the writing. Soon it became a showcase for everything new and modern in the rapidly modernizing country. The toy railroad that Perry had brought with him fascinated the Japanese, and soon they had a real one of their own. The line, built in 1872, originated in Shimbashi in Tokyo and terminated in Yokohama, not far from the present Sakuragicho Station. The new city put in the first telegraphs and telephones and boasted the first ice cream parlor. Japan's original brewery, the Spring Valley, opened in 1870, later evolved into the famous Kirin Beer. Young Yokohama was brash, rambunctious, romantic and sometimes dangerous. It was Japan's window to the world and the world's avenue into the strange and fascinating country.

One of the first European companies to set up shop was, fittingly, that quintessential English trading company Jardine Matheson from Hong Kong. The traders brought their Chinese servants and clerks with them, and they formed the beginning of the city's famous Chinatown. It is no longer the largest Chinese community in Japan, but it is still the most conspicuous and self-conscous. The main social center is the large Guan Di Temple, which dates from 1873. Several blocks are given over to Chinese restaurants that draw patrons from all over Tokyo. It is not hard to know when you are entering Chinatown. A big red gate at the entrance helpfully reads "Chinatown" on it.

Not far away on the water front is another Yokohama landmark, the Hotel New Grand. It sits behind Yamanashi Park, on what used to be called the "Bund." It still exudes quiet elegance. Sepia photographs on the wall chronicle its glory days. One shows a square-jawed Gen. Douglas MacArthur leaving the hotel trailed by a posse of aides. Perhaps he is on his way to accept Japan's surrender. It was here that the general spent his first nights in Japan. The gift shop is run by Gumps, the famous San Francisco department store, "since 1861". Somehow it seems inevitable that the parent company was purchased by the giant Tobu Department Store chain in 1991. The hotel's grand ballroom, with its high ceiling and chandeliers, is now used for wedding parties.

A little rest and fortification is advisable before beginning the climb up to the bluff. When they settled in Asia, Europeans always sought the high ground, so it wasn't long before they began to abandon their original camp on the Bund and settle among the pine trees of the wooded hills above the port. When one of his marines, Robert Williams, died on board the USS Mississippi, Perry requested a burial site overlooking the sea. This was the beginning of the Yokohama Foreign General Cemetery.

It must be said that the view from the bluff today is not one of the grandest of vistas. In the foreground is a jumble of warehouses and piers, a few ships and the new Yokohama Bay Bridge looming in the distance. The local people are supremely proud of their new bridge, which figures prominently on the cover of city brochures, and continually invites comparison with other famous spans such as the bridges across San Francisco's Golden Gate or Sydney's Harbor Bridge. It has the classic arches, and it is certainly emblematic of the city's new get-up-and-go. Yet it might be more impressive in another setting, or if it really led somewhere besides an artificial island and cargo container terminal. As it is, the bridge is merely a link, a magnificent cog, in the great looping highway around the bay.

"A dead-alive place without picturesqueness," wrote Isabella Bird, a 19th-century travel writer when she visited Yokohama in 1878. She wasted little time setting out to see the "real" Japan. There is nothing dead about Yokohama today. Europeans once amused themselves at the race track. Today the *Hamakko*, as the locals call themselves, have their own diversions: a new soccer stadium, reputedly the largest in Asia and a 59-hectare amusement park that was built on an artificial island Hakkejima in the southern part of the city. It comes complete with an escalator that leads through an aquarium and is reputedly the largest in Japan. A giant roller-coaster careers out over the harbor. In a burst of civic pride, the local professional baseball team was renamed the "Yokohama Bay Stars". Before it carried the more prosaic moniker, "Taiyo Whales".

The great trading houses of the last century have long departed the city, drawn into the orbit of Tokyo. Today, Yokohama is a branch town and bedroom community. It still trades on its name recognition and reputation as an "international" city. But it is no longer the place where everything that is new and different filters into Japan. With 3.2 million people Yokohama is Japan's second largest city. It is still a great port, packing and shipping the VCRs, refrigerators, air conditioners and automobiles to the world. Most of its residents, many of whom commute daily to jobs in the capital, are in spirit really Tokyoites. But they return each evening to a city that is less costly, less hurried, more liveable and perhaps more human.

— T.C.

---

* These names have been changed at the request of the people mentioned.

# 7

# Food

The young couple stands at the rack studying the magazine with intensity.

"How about ethnic?" he asks.

"OK, but it has to be right around here and cheap," she answers.

"Here's one, Thai, just across the street. Sounds good, but just in case we don't like the looks of it when we get there, let's choose a back up," he suggests.

They put down the *Pia Ranking* magazine and pick up a copy of *Tokyo Walker*, another of the countless catalogue-like magazines and books listing restaurants, bars and cafes in Tokyo. This week's edition features a spread on "ethnic" — the English word is used in Japanese to describe Southeast Asian food or any other spicy cuisine — restaurants in the Shinjuku district. They take a couple of minutes to evaluate the dozen or so eating spots profiled in the area, zeroing in on one. Armed with a second choice, the couple heads off for the evening's dining adventure. The magazine is immediately picked up by a pair of young women who had been trying to elbow their way up to the rack.

The scene is repeated at bookstores around Tokyo every evening as the dinner hour approaches. Eating out is the number one leisure-time activity of the capital. Hundreds of books and magazines focusing on different types of cuisine or highlighting restaurants in sections of the city cater to the hunger for dining out. Most include pictures of the dishes served, prices on the menu, descriptions of the interior decor and maps showing the locations. About 20 books make up the *Chibi Hanako* series alone, with titles like "600 Restaurants in Shinjuku" or "400 Ethnic Restaurants in Tokyo." The *Oz* mini-magazine series includes, "Cakes and Desserts: 218 Cafes," "213 Japanese Restaurants in Tokyo," and "153 Places to Eat in Takadanobaba." The "Gourmet Bible" series, aimed at a somewhat more sophisticated older crowd, includes titles like "82 Japanese Restaurants You Have to Try at Least Once" and "100 Bars Where You Can Forget Time." Tokyo diners need the help. New York proclaims itself the restaurant capital of the world, bragging about its 18,000 restaurants serving everything from steaks and sushi to soul food and Spanish cuisine. In fact, Tokyo wins by a mile — a 1996 count came up with over 109,000 eating establishments in the city. That total includes 11,000 Chinese restaurants, 2,000 Korean barbecue restaurants, 6,400 Japanese noodle shops, 6,200 Western restaurants and 9,740 coffee shops.

Food — the preparation of it, the packaging of it, the serving of it and the consuming of it — is one of Tokyo's most enduring obsessions. Not only is the print media full of food stories; switch on TV Tokyo, the local broadcast channel, and chances are a food program will appear. And not just a standard cooking show either — though there are plenty of those. Shows include "The All Time Glutton Competition: Male vs. Female," in which two people stuff themselves with noodles, sushi and gooey desserts for two hours, "Tokyo's Best Ramen Shops," where outstanding noodle shops are featured, and "Day Trips from Tokyo: Hot Spring Resorts with Gourmet Meals for Lady Travellers" appear with regularity. And pity the poor TV viewer who doesn't live in the capital. The national broadcast stations' schedules are full of food shows, too — shows that more often than not highlight and include a disproportionate number of eating places in Tokyo. At one time the most popular show in its time slot, "Iron Chef", still attracts a large audience eager to watch one chef challenge another in the preparation of an elaborate meal. The show is filmed as if it were a police show, with hand-held shots, odd angles and urgent narration. The tension builds while the judges taste and evaluate the finished product.

Even shows that, on the surface, have nothing to do with food manage to work it in on a regular basis. One of the most highly rated programs, a one-hour variety show hosted by the popular all-boy singing group SMAP, includes a half-hour cooking segment during which the singers prepare a meal for a special guest star. On a talk show hosted by a pair of comedians, guest stars are requested to bring a favorite food for the hosts to sample. In one show, "*Dochi no Ryori Sho?*" literally "Which Dish Wins?" the food is clearly the star. Celebrities are asked to decide, after an hour of mouth-watering discussion of the ingredients and watching guest chefs prepare two dishes, which of the two they would rather eat. Recent food fights included: curry pilaf vs. kimchi fried rice, rolled cabbage vs. meat loaf, and Chinese roast pork noodles vs. fried tofu over Japanese noodles. Talk about comparing apples and oranges; it wouldn't be surprising to find a future show featuring mandarin oranges vs. Fuji apples.

These shows along with the many food magazines have sparked many a food fad: the Italian dessert tiramisu, the Southeast Asian dessert nata de coco and anything "ethnic." A food fad starts when a magazine like *Hanako* features it, causing free-spending young women in search of the next best thing to run out to the nearest restaurant to sample it. In the mid-1990s, hot cocoa flew off the supermarket shelves when newspapers, magazines and TV shows carried the story that it was a cancer-preventive. In the late 1990s, red wine was the beneficiary. Sales of the drink shot up when it was reported that by drinking red wine one could be healthy and sophisticated at the same time. Then there was pepper. School girls never left home without a full pepper shaker in their purses. They sprinkled it on everything, from ice cream to noodles, after reading in a magazine that pepper could induce weight loss.

The power, importance and pervasiveness of food is nothing new, of course. From the time of teahouses, where geisha served the rich and powerful, and roadside rest stops were designed to serve lords making their way to old Edo along the Tokaido Highway, restaurants have played a central role in political life, too. Tokyo's smoke-filled rooms are not located in office buildings or hotels, as they are in other world power centers. The deals get done in private tatami rooms of high-priced *ryotei* restaurants, restaurants that are so exclusive and expensive that admission cannot be gained without an introduction even though they technically are public places. Restaurants have even been center stage in recent political scandals. Throughout Japan's modern history scandals have come and gone, but it took one related to food and drink to really make people sit up and take note. In the mid-1990s, the public learned that regional government officials from all over Japan had been routinely trekking to Tokyo to entertain officials in the central government in hopes of winning important projects or increases in budget allotments. This entertaining — popularly known as *kan-kan settai* a new coinage roughly translated as bureaucrat-to-bureaucrat wining and dining — outraged everyone. The image of civil servants living it up at the taxpayers' expense was too much to take. Stories came out revealing that the bureaucrats, previously Japan's most trusted and conservative class, were spending thousands of dollars a pop at restaurants specializing in luxurious foods and providing sexy entertainment. The most notorious of these was the "no pants *shabu-shabu*" case where it was revealed that officials dined on expensive beef dish served by waitresses wearing aprons but no underwear. Shocking, yes, but what really teed off the public was something closer to jealousy: we'll never get to taste such high quality beef.

*Sushi* was another of the high priced treats enjoyed by the bureaucrats. The raw fish dish — particularly Edo-style sushi — is one of the most instantly recognizable, uniquely Japanese foods. While the dish has gained acceptance in sophisticated capitals around the world, for most non-Japanese it remains an acquired taste. The mention of it either makes one gag or salivate in anticipation. The origins of sushi are somewhat cloudy but the story most often told is that a chef named Yohei in 18th-century Edo modified what had been a food preservation technique and came up with the idea of serving fish over vinegar-and-sugar-seasoned rice. Two styles of sushi then developed. Kansai-style, popular in western Japan, is seasoned rice packed into a dish or bowl and covered with slices of different kinds of fish, vegetables and omelet-like egg. Edo-style sushi, however, is what most people picture when they think of sushi: small balls of seasoned rice topped with a slice of fish, and a dab of *wasabi*, Japanese horse radish, holding it all together.

Over the years, sushi developed a reputation as a delicacy, an expensive treat for special occasions, so it is not surprising that the prolonged recession hit sushi shops hard. The number of shops in Tokyo has been declining steadily. There were 7,220 sushi restaurants in Tokyo in 1991, but by 1996 the number had decreased to 6,800. With its status as something of a national symbol, there is no chance that the dish will die out; however, the industry is undergoing something of a revolution. The traditional Edo-style sushi shops — shops that conform to the popular image — are struggling. First of all, they are expensive. Customers should to be prepared to drop at least $150 per person, more if they want to drink. Next, they are exclusive. Most are designed so that it is impossible to see inside before venturing in, scaring away new and less confident customers. In addition, sushi shops have their own special language — words only used in sushi restaurants when ordering tea, rice, the pickled ginger condiment and other items. Those less accustomed to the routine can be intimidated, afraid they will not be able to order correctly and will be exposed for the novices that they are. Finally, sushi shops are traditionally seen as a man's domain. Few women feel comfortable dining in a sushi shop on their own or even with female friends. Once these features spelled success, but now they are likely to lead to bankruptcy for all but the most famous and expensive places. The economic downturn has meant fewer and fewer expense-account customers, previously the bread-and-butter of the business. And the traditional sushi shop image is of no help at all in attracting the paramount consumers of the 90s and beyond — young working women.

*Sushi Magazine*, a trade publication, is trying to help shops cope. In a preface to a special feature on "Surviving the Recession," the editor exhorts his readers: "Preserving the traditions is all well and good but to survive we've got to have fresh ideas and provide a service matching the needs of modern customers." The magazine urges sushi shop owners to have a look at successful Italian and French restaurants in the city, warning, "You can't only judge what your customers want from inside your shop. You have to get out there and look around at the competition." It suggests such ideas — earth shattering to the discreet sushi traditionalist — as giving a cute name to a specially priced meal and posting a sign outside announcing it. One shop did just that and was able to lure new customers into the shop with the friendly and casual sounding "just-stopping-by meal" priced at $25, including a drink. They found that not only did it attract new customers but also that most of the new customers stayed to order additional food and drinks, spending on average more than $10 over and above the price of the original meal.

Other shops have found different strategies for success. At Sushi Umisachi, a shop in downtown Tokyo, customers regularly line up outside, waiting up to an hour at peak times, for one of 32 seats. The shop's sushi is cheap, with prices ranging from just 40 cents to $3.30 a piece, and the serving size is generous. But the most attractive feature for many customers is that Sushi Umisachi has eliminated the element of fear. Order slips, kept outside the door, list all the available items. While they wait, customers write down their orders, choosing what they want from the posted menus and plastic food models. No chance exists of making a faux pas, and by the time they reach their seats, their sushi will be there waiting for them.

The most revolutionary idea to hit the sushi world in the past few years, however, is *kaiten zushi*, or conveyor belt sushi. Customers sit at a brightly-lit counter, watching as the sushi glides by on the belt, two pieces to a plate. This is the ultimate in a non-threatening sushi experience. No words are necessary. You see what you like and you reach out and grab it. There's no mystery about the price either. Customers pay according to the number of plates stacked up in front of them when they are finished. When kaiten zushi shops first started appearing in Tokyo in the late 1980s, they were seen as little more than a gimmick. They could no more compete with real sushi shops than McDonald's could compete with a Kansas City steak house. They were cheap, but customers got what they paid for. Now the tables have been turned. In 1998, out of the total sushi sales of $125 billion, $40 billion, or almost one-third, came from kaiten zushi. Analysts predict that it is only a matter of time before the industry takes the lead.

Kaisen Misakiko, in Tokyo's Meguro district, is an industry leader. The headline of *Sushi Magazine's* feature on the shop says it all: "Creating a shop that makes young women customers feel at home results in monthly sales of $250,000 for this 42-seat restaurant!" About 60 percent of Kaisen Misakiko's customers are women and apparently the key to attracting them is glass windows, a bright interior and value for the money. There are five different price levels, ranging from 90 cents to 3.90 per plate of two pieces, with choices ranging from the usual raw tuna and squid to the creative breaded fried shrimp roll and crab cole slaw sushi. Even desserts like fruit and pudding sundaes glide by on the belt. The shop has another popular feature: a two-level conveyor belt, the latest innovation. The top level carries the sushi while ceramic cups for tea circulate below.

But Tokyo is not all raw fish. The variety of food available is staggering and the growth in the number of restaurants serving non-Japanese food has been explosive. In the early 1980s, before the Bubble Era, foreign food in Tokyo was relatively hard to come by: a handful of Italian restaurants, a few haughty French establishments, several friendly Indian restaurants and one tiny Mexican place. This is not to say that Western food was unknown in Tokyo. In fact, just as other elements of Western society, like Western-style dress, were imported wholesale during the Meiji Period, Western food came to Japan, too. Before Meiji, the Japanese diet, following Buddhist beliefs, did not generally include meat of any kind. Then beef, pork and dairy products were introduced and a whole new genre of restaurants was born, known simply as Western restaurants. Some of these restaurants still survive, serving their uniquely Japanese versions of Western food, exotic to the Japanese, but generally unrecognizable to Westerners.

One of the oldest is Rengatei, established in 1896, in Ginza. The name, literally "brick restaurant," refers to the Meiji Era red brick used to rebuild the district after it was destroyed by fire in 1872. Until it was once again destroyed in the Great Earthquake of 1923, the area was the epitome of sophistication, with its two-story brick buildings, paved sidewalks, gaslights and horse drawn streetcars. Crowds flocked to Ginza to window shop, stroll and, of course, eat, just as they do today. Stepping in to sample the Western fare at places like Rengatei was considered de riguer. Today, Rengatei still stands close to the main intersection, on Ginza Gaslight Road. Although the building has been rebuilt several times, the menu has hardly changed. The restaurant claims to have introduced the breaded pork cutlet to Japan and to have been the first to have paired it with shredded cabbage. This pairing was fateful: just as pickled ginger must always be served with sushi, pork cutlet must always be served with shredded cabbage. It's as hard and fast a rule as the one about taking your shoes off when you enter a house.

In the little over 100 years since these Western dishes were introduced in Tokyo, they have entered the consciousness and found a home. Curry rice, Hayashi rice (gravy over rice first served by Mr. Hayashi in the tiny restaurant on the top floor of Maruzen department store in Nihonbashi), *omu*-rice (a thin egg crepe artfully wrapped around a crescent-shaped mound of rice — with some ketchup drizzled over it) and corn potage, for years the only Western soup available in Japan — are all comfort foods in today's Japan. Ironically, these are the home-cooked Japanese meals boomers' dream of when they miss their moms' cooking.

Some dishes that started out in the Western eateries were, over the years, elevated to the status of genuine Japanese dishes and they earned a real name written in real Japanese letters, as opposed to the katakana syllabary reserved for foreign loan words. *Tonkatsu* is one such dish. Near relative to the breaded pork cutlet, tonkatsu broke out of the pack and now is served in restaurants devoted to serving nothing else, except maybe breaded deep fried prawn now and then.

Tonki, one of the most popular and oldest tonkatsu specialty restaurants in Tokyo, is something of a shrine to the dish. At its main branch in Meguro, just across the tracks from the profitable kaiten zushi place, the forty seats are spaced around a U-shaped counter. The decor is sparse, the counter, the seats and the floors all blond wood, reminiscent of the quiet elegance of the national Shinto shrine in Ise. The counter seats surround the staging area where a team of chefs and assistants — all dressed in white — each perform their assigned tasks. Two young men do nothing but dip lean pork cutlets into flour, egg and breadcrumbs in that order three times each. Another young man plunges the prepared cutlets into the vats of hot oil and tends them. When they are perfectly browned, he transfers them to the slicing station where an older man cuts the finished tonkatsu into inch-thick slices for easy chopstick handling. Meanwhile, another worker has been preparing the plates, piling them with the obligatory mountain of shredded cabbage, slice of tomato, scoop of potato salad and dab of hot mustard.

Standing in the center, directing the action and greeting customers is the owner, Koki Yochihara. In his mid-70s, Yochihara took over the operation from his father, who began selling tonkatsu from an outdoor food stall before World War II, more than 60 years ago. Several branches throughout the city now bear the same Tonki name and are operated by relatives or former staff at the original. They performed their apprenticeships so well that they are permitted to use the name. While the food is the main attraction at Tonki, Yochihara's technique as a maitre d' is also well known. When all the counter seats are taken, Yochihara calls out to new customers as they enter asking for their order. He makes a brief notation and asks them to take a seat anywhere on the benches lining the wall. There is no need to sit in line; Yochihara never confuses an order or fails to call customers to take their seats at the counter in the correct order. A full meal at Tonki is cheap. It costs about $13 for a boneless cutlet, miso soup, pickles and all the rice and shredded cabbage one can eat. Nevertheless, the recession has had its effects. "Our customers are still coming, but they are coming less often. When they used to come two or three times a month, now it's only once or twice," explains Yochihara. "But we're not changing anything. We're going to keep doing what we've always done."

Exactly the sentiments of some brave coffee shop owners in Tokyo. The coffee shop is another Tokyo institution dating from the Meiji era. The first ones opening in the 1880s in Ueno, provided places to sample the sophisticated drink. Post-war, they grew into a cross between a European café, where the price of a cup bought the customer a place to relax and a smoke-filled rest lounge where tired workers could catch a few winks on the boss's time. In typical Tokyo fashion, coffee shop owners began to specialize: classical music coffee shops, comic book coffee shops, fine ceramic coffee shops and even "no-pants" coffee shops (the waitresses, not the customers). The one thing the coffee shops had in common was the quality of the coffee and the price of a cup: both very high. A cup of coffee in a traditional Tokyo coffee shop was about $5 — without refills.

Then came Doutor, the first fast-food styled coffee chain in Japan. Doutor opened its first franchise shop in 1980 with the philosophy of "satisfying more customers with a high quality product." Clearly fulfilling a need for a cheap ($1.15) no-frills cup of coffee, there are now 764 shops nation-wide, the company posting a growth rate of 50.9 percent in fiscal 1996. Atmosphere and comfort were sacrificed for speed and economy. The seats are narrow, self-service is the rule, and if the cigarette smoke doesn't overpower you, the scent of the bathroom air freshener will. But Doutor has filled a need and it, along with its imitators, has had a profound effect on the old style coffee shops. Their numbers declined from 12,400 in 1991 to 9,740 in 1996, a drop of 21.5 percent.

But still some owners uphold the honor of the old coffee shop. Dug, a jazz coffee shop in Shinjuku, has got the atmosphere almost too right. In Tokyo, you don't do something if you aren't going to do it right. And doing it right means fulfilling, down to the last detail, the romantic image of whatever it is you're trying to do. For Dug's owner, Nakadaira Kaoru, it is jazz. At Dug, you don't mind the cigarette smoke, in fact you welcome it. The exposed brick walls, the dark wood floors and counter, the etched glass lampshades in amber, pink and green create the perfect, but still unstudied, mood. It comes as no surprise at all to see the customer in the darkest corner with a goatee and beret enjoying his freshly brewed $6 cup of Colombian and digging the cool jazz. At Tajima-ya, also in the Shinjuku district, the object is to recreate the feel of a 1920s Tokyo coffee shop. Set in an old (for Shinjuku: the 1950s) building, the shop opened in the late 1980s. The natural wood interior, the "antiques" decorating the room and the china and ceramic cups displayed around the shop create a homey atmosphere. The menu includes such items as cold white chocolate drink for $5.40 and Mocha Mettai #4 Yemen coffee for $6.

Cafe L'Ambre in Ginza is a true Tokyo institution: a shop devoted to coffee and coffee alone, as is noted sternly on the sign outside. This is a shop for serious drinkers. The menu divides the offerings into quality categories: silver, gold, reserve, extra reserve and beans over ten years old. Prices range from $5.80 to $10.80 per cup. And there are strict rules: certain types of coffee must be drunk black. If a customer wants to add milk he or she must order a different type or leave. L'Ambre is run by a family of coffee cultists who opened the shop in 1948. Dad still hand roasts the beans in an ancient machine in the front window, while Mom and Son brew the coffee cup-by-cup. This is true dedication. "It's tough to survive in today's atmosphere, but we're not in the business to get rich. We just love coffee. It's true there are plenty of people who like to drink coffee, but people who really love coffee and can appreciate it are rare today. But these are the people we want for our customers," explains the serious son.

The specialist coffee shop seems doomed in the Tokyo of the early 21st century but perhaps if L'Ambre can stick it out, they'll have a chance. As successful as the fast food-like Doutor has been, even they are beginning to re-think their concept in the face of competition from overseas. Starbucks came to Tokyo in 1996 and by the end of 1998 had over 50 outlets. The French franchise Deux Magots has also licensed franchises, straight from Paris. Escargots are served. The relaxed atmosphere, the bigger space and the variety of the coffee available attracted the free-spending young women customers, who had begun to shun Doutor. In response, Doutor opened Le Cafe Doutor. Right at the main Ginza intersection and in sharp contrast to other Doutor outlets, the new shop is open, airy and suspiciously like a traditional relaxing coffee shop. What comes around in Tokyo, definitely goes around.

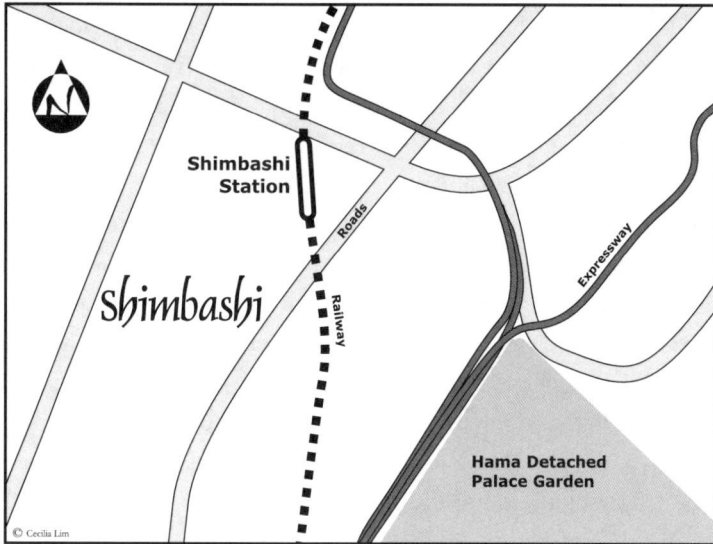

## Mingling with the Masses in Shimbashi

When the Tokyo TV newscasters want a man-on-the-street opinion for their nightly news shows, they usually head for Shimbashi, a second-tier business district, just off Ginza. Come nine or ten o'clock at night, you are certain to find crowds of tipsy salarymen leaving the thousands of tiny restaurants and bars, making their way across the plaza to the train station with tongues just loose enough to bravely venture an opinion.

Shimbashi, a prime geisha and entertainment district since the Meiji Era, has been in its present state since the Occupation, when small out-door eateries sprang up along the elevated railroad tracks. The bars and restaurants serve cheap but filling snacks like *yakitori* or grilled chicken on skewers, *ramen* or noodles in soup, and other side dishes suitable to accompany beer or sake — the real main attraction after all — to give the weary working man a casual place to stop in before heading home. While there has been some redevelopment, the 1950s-Japan flavor of the area has been largely unchanged.

It's still very much a man's world, as Miki Igari explained to me. "I would never come here with just a couple of girlfriends," she said as we settled onto our seats at the counter at Torihana, a yakitori shop with seating for just fifteen — ten seats at the counter and two tables. "It's not that it's taboo or that we wouldn't be allowed in, it's just that we wouldn't feel comfortable." Masaharu, Miki's husband and a Torihana regular agreed, explaining that this place, just like Shimbashi in general was not fashionable and that he liked it for that very reason. "It's comfortable; it's honest; no one is pretending to be anything they are not."

Our fellow diners at the counter looked like they had been recruited by central casting: three red-faced salarymen in their late forties, ties loosened, tongues thickened. They had started early and although it was only 6:30 when we arrived, they were already deep into a drunken discussion about company restructuring and the effects of the recession. We clearly had some catching up to do. As is usual in yakitori shops, we ordered by simply telling the owner/chef behind the counter what we didn't want. For Miki and me, it was no chicken skin and no organs. We were prepared for anything else. As is customary, we started with draft beer and then progressed to chilled sake.

The chef handed our yakitori over the counter, skewer by skewer as it was ready. One by one they came: baby green peppers stuffed with minced chicken, white meat chicken bits coated in a sweet soy-based sauce, chicken wrapped in shiso-leaf, pepper-coated asparagus, grilled baby onion with garlic chips, ginger eggplant, and salted, grilled ginkgo nuts. Between skewers we cleansed our palates with finely grated *daikon* radish mixed with grated ginger and soy sauce — every bit as tasty and effective as the sorbet served between courses in fancy French restaurants.

Though the yakitori had been filling, for Miki and Masaharu it wasn't enough. In Japan, yakitori alone does not a meal make. For one thing, it doesn't come with rice or soup. Something more was needed, they felt, and I followed along. Back out on the narrow street there were several tempting possibilities. As we walked along, Masaharu pointing out his favorite spots (This was the third night in a row that he'd been drinking and eating in the Shimbashi district.), we heard the sounds of a *shamisen*, a guitar-like traditional Japanese instrument. I assumed it was taped music coming from one of the restaurants until I turned around and saw a man of about 80, dressed in kimono, strumming a shamisen strolling up the street. "He's here just about every night — not playing for money, just for the fun of it. I'm sure you'll only see that in Shimbashi these days," Masaharu told me.

We decided to have ramen and entered a funky old shop with oil lanterns hanging outside and a sign proclaiming: "We use the recipe that my 82 year-old grandfather used." The noodles were hot and filling and tasty enough to satisfy the customers, who all, like us, had done a fair amount of drinking at a previous spot.

Warmed and satisfied, we left the restaurant, joined the lurching crowd and wove our way to the station. Another night out on the town, Tokyo-style.

— S.F.M

# 8

# Fun

Call it bad PR or just a lack of information, but Tokyo does not have a reputation as a "fun" place. Most foreign media reports focus on the economy — not usually a fun topic — and when Tokyo appears on the TV news, the most often used image is a crowd of grim-faced businessmen emerging from Tokyo Station heading off to another day of office drudgery.

In fact, nothing could be further from the truth. In Tokyo they take their "fun" very seriously. Longtime Tokyo resident and scholar, Donald Richie was once asked why the Japanese bothered to franchise a branch of Disneyland. Tokyo, he said, is one mammoth amusement park, with an area of 2,500 sq. km and a staff of almost 12 million. Bangkok's Patpong, Seoul's Itaewon, Hong Kong's Lan Kwai Fong and even New York's Times Square all pale in comparison to Tokyo's several entertainment districts, all with their own special appeal. Ginza, with hostess bars, expensive Western restaurants and sushi shops, caters to the businessman on an expense account. Akasaka, close to the government offices and the seat of power, provides private, exclusive and discreet teahouses for entertaining. Shibuya appeals to the younger set, offering cheap bars and all-you-can-eat joints. Aoyama is for the sophisticated, upscale and artistic — featuring jazz clubs, fusion restaurants and celebrity watching. Roppongi is the haunt of the foreign community with discos, karaoke pubs and the Hard Rock Café.

But it Shinjuku's Kabukicho that is the ultimate Tokyo playground. The neon, the noise and the crowds are unrivalled. Many ordinary Tokyo residents avoid the area, labelling it dangerous because it is filled with pachinko halls, massage parlors, sex related businesses, and the gangsters and touts who operate those places. But to a visitor from any other country where a dangerous neighborhood is one where you are likely to get mugged or shot, Kabukicho resembles nothing less than "Viceland" as might be imagined and produced by Disney and Co.

Flattened by the Allied bombing of 1945, Shinjuku became the site of a large post-war gangster-controlled black market. Hoping to give the area a lift after the war, officials proposed rebuilding the destroyed Kabuki Theater in the district and, in anticipation, the section of Shinjuku to the northeast of the station was named Kabukicho. In the end, the theater was rebuilt on its original site in Ginza, but the name Kabukicho, which literally means "Kabuki Town", stuck and the gangsters stayed on, too.

Kabukicho's gangsters are straight out of central casting, circa 1955, right off the set of "Guys and Dolls." They all have the requisite pinstripe suits, tightly permed hair and aviator sunglasses. Scar optional. Underlings who act as touts for the many hostess clubs have long straight hair, wear plum-colored double-breasted suits and gold jewelry. Their cartoon-character look, combined with the fact that they rarely bother "civilians" or carry guns makes them more a part of the entertainment than a threat to casual visitors.

The sex clubs seem like parodies of sex clubs, too. There are peeping clubs, where customers spy on the girls through one-way mirrors or holes in the wall; "image clubs," where the girls dress up in fantasy costumes (nurses, teachers, schools girls, stewardesses, popular cartoon characters); lingerie bars (staff in underwear); no-pants bars (staff in no underwear); married women pubs (all the hostesses are married); host bars (for women customers); "dandy" bars (for women, but the "hosts" are women in drag). The permutations are endless.

And then there are the love hotels, found in the back streets of Shinjuku, Shibuya and entertainment districts throughout Tokyo. Few things have done more to add spice to contemporary Tokyo's architectural stew than the design and decor of these palaces. For it is not enough merely to provide a discreet and convenient hideaway where a politician can while away an hour or two with a favorite mistress, where a bar hostess can take a client or where young couples can find moments of privacy. No, the imagination must be stimulated and the senses appeased. Thus, one finds buildings scattered throughout the capital that look like Bavarian castles or space ships or ocean liners. The interiors are equally exotic with blood red carpets, ersatz Italian furniture, revolving beds, mirrors, even cartoon figures painted on the wall, depending on one's taste.

Some of the more outlandish designs have fallen out of fashion in recent years, and most of the establishments in the back streets of Kabukicho are less garish now. They seem to alternate between mock-Greek, complete with cupid statues in the front, to shiny, space-ship gray cylinders. It is said that as many as 50 million Japanese patronize love hotels every year, which would seem to suggest that there is a lot of philandering going on. Or maybe not. Many people use these places for other reasons. Some are married couples wanting to get away from children or in-laws for a few hours. Indeed, it has become fashionable now to call them "leisure hotels" or "boutique hotels."

But Kabukicho is not all sex. There are legitimate movie theaters, discos, restaurants and thousands of cheap drinking places, making it a popular gathering spot for college students, too. Students from the prestigious rival universities of Keio and Waseda repair to Kabukicho after the big game to celebrate victory or to drown their sorrows after defeat. The tendency for some students in a drunken stupor to take the drowning part too literally was one reason why city officials decided to pave over a large fountain in the heart of the district. There were too many unfortunate incidents involving drunk students.

For those seeking more wholesome entertainment, Tokyo abounds with theme parks of all descriptions. Early parks were fairly crude affairs, perhaps an "international village" with replicas of a Dutch townhouse or an African village hut. Now the capital is dotted with larger, more sophisticated versions, and new ones seem to open every other week. Tokyo Disneyland is the most successful park in the world. Since it opened in 1983, more than 200 million people have passed through its gates, and the numbers continued to increase even during the recession years that set in after the Bubble burst. This is despite the fairly steep $40 entry pass. About 15 million people go there — not all of them on one day, although it may seem like it. When the park opened in 1983 many wondered whether the Japanese would take to the place. After all, it is virtually identical to Disney World in Florida with almost no concessions to local culture, other than the fact that Mickey and Minnie Mouse wear kimonos during the New Year's parade. They may have underestimated the Tokyoites' passion for packaged escapism or their ability to assimilate foreign culture and make it their own.

By now millions of children have visited the Magic Kingdom, and they hardly think of it as being American at all. Pluto and company have become as familiar and as Japanese to them as Hello Kitty, which also has a theme park. It has been such a success that the company is planning a huge expansion called DisneySea on 71 hectares on the southeastern end of the park. It has, obviously, an aquatic theme, with attractions such as Mermaid lagoon and 20,000 Leagues Under the Sea. The park manager estimates that the combined parks will draw a staggering 25 million visitors a year. But it is only one of a half a dozen other big parks planned along Tokyo Bay. They include the Danish Legoland near Makuhari and Osama Tezuka World, dedicated to one of the country's greatest manga comic artists.

Many of the newer parks cater to a Japanese desire to see the world without having to leave the safety of the home islands. The most famous of this genre, a replica of Holland, however, is in southern Japan. Others stroke a growing nostalgia for the past. As mentioned, almost nothing is left in Tokyo that is much older than the Taisho period of the 1920s. To discover what life was like in the distant or sometimes not-so-distant past, people can visit all kinds of restored villages, such as the Edo-Tokyo Tatemonoen in the western suburbs. This is an open-air architectural museum boasting dozens of original period buildings moved there from their original locations closer to the city center. Nostalgia isn't always enough to make a park successful, though. Ofuna Cinema World outside of Kamakura, centered around Tora-san, the character in the longest-running film series in Japanese history, opened in 1995 and closed in 1998. Nostalgia for Kiyoshi Atsumi, the actor who played Tora-san, evidently did not survive his death.

One of the most spectacular successful of these genre parks is a modest establishment in Yokohama that is dedicated to celebrating, of all things, the lowly bowl of ramen noodles. Ramen is the salaryman's quick, cheap, filling lunch, loved by Japanese all over. The basic bowl is a broth flavored with soy sauce, and garnished with roast pork, bamboo stems and a large sheet of dried seaweed. It is said to have been invented in China and imported to Japan in 1165. The first ramen noodle shop opened in the capital in 1910. This charming museum opens with display walls lined with different packages of instant ramen and bowls from famous noodle shops. Even the English captions display a certain poetry, as in this one: "As the charumera flute plays the melancholic melody 'so-la-si-la-sol' which drifts through the air, the mobile ramen stand strolls through the streets in the night so cold that even the stars freeze over. And that was the beginning of it all."

The lower two floors have been turned into a replica of a typical Tokyo street at dusk. The year is 1958, a seminal year in noodledom since it was the year of the invention of the instant ramen, the "greatest postwar invention" in Japan the museum modestly notes. One enters through a railway station gate, the ticket taker chanting and snapping his punch, the kind who has all but disappeared from every Tokyo station these days. The darkened alleyway is lined with cubby-hole bars, a couple of them real, plus the entrance to a public bathhouse and a movie house, and posters of Godzilla and Toshiro Mifune wielding a sword in a 1950s samurai epic. One hears again the joyful cry of "*kami shibai*" as an itinerant story teller pulls up his bicycle and starts telling children stories with sliding paper pictures from the back of his bike. It is a time before the arrival of McDonalds, Kentucky Fried Chicken and or even conveyor-belt sushi. For many young visitors, it is a time as distant and quaint as colonial Williamsburg is for Americans.

But the real draw is ramen. There are the six real ramen noodle shops, each one featuring a particular style of ramen from Kyushu to Hokkaido, selected from over 1,000 throughout Japan that the museum staff have actually traveled to and checked out. Lines of people stretch as visitors wait to buy their $10 ticket and take a seat around the crowded counter to receive a heaping bowl-full. Some try out two or three at a time, while others come back repeatedly. One can buy a season pass and it seems like a far more popular place than some of Tokyo's more prestigious institutions. Indeed, the Ramen Museum is said to draw more visitors annually then the National Museum of Art.

Some theme parks reflect one of the ideas behind traditional Japanese gardens, that nature can be mimicked, improved upon and enhanced with meticulous planning. Why join the crowds flying to Phuket when Wild Blue Yokohama, an artificial indoor beach, beckons just a short train ride away? No matter what the weather or the season, visitors can surf, swim and even "sunbathe" under the dome. One day at the beach, the next on the slopes. In suburban Funabashi, the giant hump of the LaLaport Skidome, the world's largest indoor ski slope, juts up some 25 stories, offering customers a 490-meter run down a course of artificial snow. To produce the snow, a mix of fine water mist and compressed air is sprayed onto the slope from 94 nozzles mounted in the ceiling catwalk. The system produces ultra-fine powder snow crystals some 80 microns in diameter. Of course, the steel girders that hold up the ceiling and the gray walls on the sides may not quite match up with the vistas provided by the Japan Alps. But aside from their all-year convenience and proximity, these huge indoor amusement parks seem to fulfil a deep Japanese desire for a well-ordered world. It is a world where the snow is more real than can be found in real life, where there are no moguls or ice spots to send the skier tumbling, where there are no sunburns or insect bites to worry about at the beach.

For those who want to have fun but would rather not even get wet, there is the entirely virtual experience. In the center of urban Shibuya and on the top floors of the classy Takashimaya department store in Shinjuku, the game maker Sega operates Joypolis, a game center filled with virtual reality attractions. At the Wild River ride, the tension builds during the 40-minute wait in line. Passengers waiting to board the large rubber raft watch scenes from their upcoming white water adventure and are subjected to repeated warnings. Those with weak hearts, high blood pressure or other life-threatening conditions are prohibited from taking the trip. As they reach the front of the line they are told that they must store their mobile phones, shopping bags and backpacks in waterproof containers. Just before boarding, a guide explains the risks once again. Finally, twelve at a time, they take their seats in the raft. The lights dim, the raft lurches forward and a surging river flowing though a jungle fills the 180-degree screen in the riders' line of vision. The actual raft rolls and pitches as it speeds down the virtual river, plunging down 90 degree waterfalls, hitting rocks, capsizing and flying out of control. As a finale, the craft flys through the forest, hitting trees and finally smashes into solid rock face, presumably killing all the passengers.

Other attractions include the Jurassic Park Lost World ride, where players get to shoot dinosaurs — if you miss the beast approaches and "breathes" hot air in your face — and the Murder Lodge, where participants are made to feel that they may become the victim of a horrible crime at any moment. The visitor enters a snowy mountain cabin with a table prepared for dinner, as the horror story unfolds. They huddle around the table as the host smashes dishes and the killer bangs at the door to get in, seats shaking in verisimilitude.

Game centers in Tokyo are serious business — this is not your ordinary video arcade. No longer content to shoot aliens or manipulate characters on a screen around obstacles, customers at Tokyo's arcades want to be the central figures in the games. Using a machine called "Ski Champ," players step into a pair of skis, grab the ski poles and make their way down the video slope, avoiding boulders, trees and other skiers, by leaning and shifting their weight just as they would do on a real slope. At Dance Dance Revolution, players drop a couple ¥100 coins into the slot and climb aboard a small platform. They try to match the movements of a digitized figure on the screen in front of him while techno pop blares out. The machine rates dancing skills. "Perfect," announces the computerized voice, or "boooo." Guitar Freak is a similar "game," only instead of hopping around on a lit disco floor, players take up the full size electric guitar attached to the machine and try to play along, following the notes on the screen. There also are skate board games, roller blade games and even horse racing games that similarly provide the thrills of the sports without the risks or inconvenience.

The predecessor of the game center, the pachinko parlor, is still thrives in Tokyo. Pachinko, a game played on what looks something like an upright pinball machine, was first introduced in the 1930s as a children's amusement. The machines were wheeled out and set up along with other games for children like the ring toss and goldfish hunt at neighborhood festivals. It wasn't until just after World War II, when there were few other diversions, that pachinko parlors became popular places for adults to pass the time. By the 1960s, the parlors were the haunts of salarymen. The loud martial music, the constant clang of pachinko balls cascading through the machines and the possibility of winning small prizes combined to block out the stress of the real world. Pachinko has always had a sleazy reputation. Many parlors are owned and operated by gangsters or other questionable types; professional players project something less than a professional image; and, the parlors themselves are smoke-filled and dirty. Falling out of favor somewhat during the Bubble Era (Pachinko was too cheap a pastime for those high-living years.), it came back with a vengeance in the late 1990s, as smart pachinko parlor owners started to repackage the places in an effort to "image up," as they say in Japanese.

Newer, brighter parlors started opening in smart neighborhoods. Some parlors installed love seats so that couples could play together; some began to serve food and drinks, others offered designer goods as prizes. The games themselves also went modern: replacing the old noisy mechanical machines were digital versions of the game board. The balls still jangle through and a winning game is still measured by the number of metal ball-bearing sized balls a player ends up with, but the pachinko machine itself looks more like an electronic slot machine or video game. The game has its fanatics who line up outside popular parlors hours before opening time to make sure that they secure their favorite machine — the one with the big payoff. For, while the scholars explain the attraction of pachinko as "a place where people can forget the worries of life and enter a virtual world where they know if they are winners and losers at the flick of a wrist," the real bottom line is money. Although pachinko parlors only offer small prizes like cigarettes or bottles of perfume to winners, everyone knows that his winning chit can be exchanged for cool hard cash at a not so discreet exchange window around the corner. The possibility of winning money is the lure, so great a lure that the pachinko industry takes in about $185 billion a year, as much as the automobile industry in Japan.

Try as they might, though, pachinko parlors still have not achieved the coveted status of "date spot" — a cool place to visit on a date, the height of fun for young singles. Unlike in the U.S. where a date is a simple evening out usually involving dinner and a movie, the Tokyo date is a complex affair. Trend magazines constantly offer advice on "date courses," that is, a series of popular or romantic spots that together make up a date sure to impress. *Tokyo Walker*, a weekly magazine aimed at the college crowd, devoted 20 pages to comparing the merits of Yokohama vs. Odaiba as date spots. The article offered two date courses for each area, economy class and executive class, recommended activities, and itemizes the costs hour by hour. The economy class Odaiba date runs from $50 a person and includes public transportation, lunch, dinner, a snack at McDonalds, relaxing on the beach, browsing at hip shops, a moonlight cruise and a couple of hours at a love hotel in down-market Asakusa. The executive class date presumes a car, costs the serious suitor about $300 per person, and concludes with a night at the swanky Hotel Grand Meridian. Cheapskates are referred to the "super economy class". The Yokohama course, which only costs about $18, including all the elements in the Odaiba economy date, except, instead of heading to a love hotel, the couple ends up making out on a bench in Yamashita Park.

Each date course is described in meticulous detail, including what to order at which restaurants — at the executive Yokohama course lunch restaurant, it's the rotisserie-grilled chicken with rosemary — ensuring no faux pas and maximum fun. Even the best and trendiest parking lots (parking lots not parking spots!) are described including photos of the lots, some patrons and their cars.

Detailed advice is not only on offer for couples: another magazine offers advice for a girls-day-out Ginza shopping expedition. One recommended route: meet at 11:00 a.m. at the main Ginza intersections, preferably in front of Wako Department Store; 11:10 a.m. proceed to the H20 counter at Matsuzakaya to check out the new line of make-up; 12 noon lunch at Sazaby's Afternoon Tea Room; 1:30 p.m. check out Vivitix, a store selling accessories and "character goods," a good place to stock up on everything Hello Kitty; 3:00 p.m. time for afternoon tea at Rive Gauche; 4:30 p.m. browse in the gourmet shop Marriage Freres; 6:00 p.m. dinner at Ginza 300 where everything on the menu is 300 yen (about $2.50). The perfect fun day, by the book.

One of the most unusual date spots is the Umihotaru rest stop in the middle of Tokyo Bay. It was erected about half-way across the water to serve the new Aqualine automobile under-water expressway. Like a lot of Bubble Era projects, Aqualine, which opened in December 1997, is a flop. To be sure, it significantly cuts the time needed to drive from Kanagawa to Kisarazu (assuming one wants to drive from Kanagawa to Kisarazu), but the hefty $45 toll one-way dampens patronage. But the five-story rest stop — there are four restaurants, all specializing in seafood, naturally, a games arcade and several souvenir shops — is a big hit with the dating crowd.

Tokyo boasts hundreds of museums, and the choice of subjects is extraordinary. In addition to museums dedicated to Japanese swords, sumo wrestling, kites, tabi or split toe socks, Noh masks and calligraphy, others are devoted to unexpected things like subways or tombstones. The Tobacco and Salt Museum in Shibuya is maintained by the government tobacco monopoly, so there is nothing bad to learn about smoking there. Among the attractions: "Famous tobacco lovers in Japanese history" and an enticing 30-minute film called, "Our Lives and Salt." A separate Cigarette Lighter Museum is located in another part of the city. There are at least two museums that display comic books. There is a museum for fireworks and another for fire. Of course, Tokyo hosts a baseball hall of fame, but it also has a museum devoted to softball. The Shaving Culture Museum displays implements going back to the Stone Age (but no electric razors). A Museum of Dry Cleaning and Laundering draws 2,500 people a year. But certainly the most unusual museum in Tokyo, maybe the world, is the Meguro Parasitological Museum, the world's only public museum devoted to parasites. The star attraction is an 8.8-meter tapeworm taken from a man who ate raw fish from the Japan Sea in 1986. Now we're talking fun.

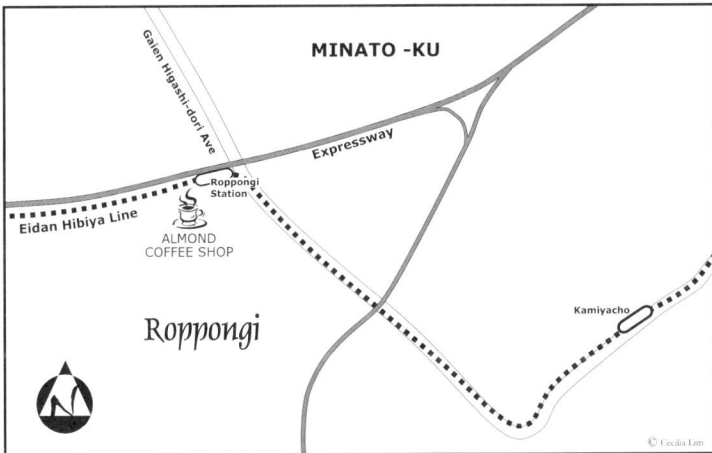

*Almond, Friday 7:00 p.m.*

Getting off the Hibiya line subway at Roppongi, I take my place among the crowd standing outside *Almond*, which the Japanese pronounce *Aa-mon-doh*. At 7:00 on a Friday evening, this is a crowded spot. About 50 of us are here outside the distinctive pink-and-white striped cafe, perfectly situated at the main Roppongi intersection. We are not waiting for tables or to buy some cream filled pastry — no one who knows better ever actually goes inside

Almond. We are here because this is where we are meeting our friends for a night on the town. Almond is one of those designated meeting points that can be found in every entertainment district in Tokyo. In the Shinjuku district, it's under the Studio Alta electronic screen; in Shibuya, near the statue of the faithful dog Hachiko (Often there are so many people waiting nearby that poor Hachiko disappears from view.); and, in Roppongi the undisputed meeting spot is outside Almond. So I join the crowd.

Time goes by quickly as I wait for my friends to arrive — the passing crowd and my fellow waiters provide the entertainment. A couple of suited businessmen wait next to two teenage girls in micro-minis, with frosted gray hair, eight-inch platform sandals and faces with that fresh-from-the tanning-salon sheen. Across the sidewalk is a pair of college-age boys with dreadlocks, baggy streetwise sweats and pierced eyebrows standing next to a group of American Wall-Street types. A trio of kimono-clad ladies scurries past on their way home from a pottery exhibition at a nearby museum. Part-timers working for various night clubs, discos and bars hand out tissue-packet advertisements and flyers, while longhaired young men in cheap tuxedos try to get attractive young women to patronize certain clubs or telephone chat lines. This is a busy place.

The district is home to more bars, restaurants, nightclubs and discos than anywhere else in Japan. The name Roppongi, or "six trees", belies the reality. This is hardly a tranquil spot. The dominant feature of the landscape is the overhead expressway. Visits in daylight are not recommended as the only memorable thing a daytime visitor is likely to note is the stench of stale beer coming from the dirty bar rugs hung out to dry after the previous night's partying. But this was once a pastoral place — the site of the estates of six Tokugawa lords, each of whom had the character for tree in his name, resulting in the name of Roppongi for the district.

At the end of the Edo period, the land was taken away from the Tokugawas and became the military drill grounds for the new Imperial army. The War College was also located there until the U.S. Army took over the area in 1945. When the troops left in 1959, Roppongi became the site of the Japan Defense Agency.

Since the days of the American military presence, the area has had a reputation as an international district. Close to Azabu, home to many diplomats and expatriates, Roppongi developed a reputation as a sophisticated, hip place to play. In contrast to the Ginza, the district where businessmen entertain each other on expense accounts, Roppongi was the place where stars, models, foreigners and other glamorous types could see and be seen.

Its reputation grew from the time the subway station opened in 1964 up until the mid-1990s, when it began to look a little tired, and the Tokyo club scene started to shift. The Roppongi crowd got younger and younger. While the turn of the century still finds it a busy place, it has become somewhat raucous, raunchy and déclassé.

Roppongi is now filled with bars like Gas Panic, where all drinks are $3.50, and there is no cover charge. Staff patrol the room making sure that customers continue to refresh their drinks, enforcing the policy displayed on the huge sign over the bar: "Customers must be drinking at all times." The policy seems designed to ensure bar fights, especially when the customer mix is mainly young, flirty Japanese women and young, possessive foreign men.

The reputation of the place has declined so much that my Japanese friends had to be persuaded to meet there for a few drinks. "I remember when I was a college student in the '70s, and I used to fantasize about going to bars in Roppongi. It was the epitome of sophistication for me — movie stars, foreigners. It was something to aspire to. Now it's sleazy, filled with teenagers, looking for a cheap beer and a cheap date. The really cool people have moved on to Aoyama," one friend told me.

It's true that the district has come down in the world, but my friend may have been saying more about himself than Roppongi. I still enjoy standing outside Almond watching the passing parade.

— S.F.M.

# 9

# Pretensions

Tokyo claims that it belongs to a select group of "world-class cities," by which it means New York, London and Paris, and no one else. But those cities are universally known for a wealth of artistic splendor not immediately associated with Japan's capital, despite its long tradition in the visual arts. Paris would not be Paris without the Louvre Museum and the Pompidou Center. New York has the Metropolitan and Guggenheim. London the Tate and the National Gallery. And Tokyo? Of course, there has been a National Museum in Tokyo's Ueno Park since 1937. It possesses some important Japanese works of art, but it is a rather conservative and dowdy institution. In the same park can be found the National Museum of Western Art. Its entire collection would probably fill little more than one room of the Louvre. During the Bubble Era years, when Japanese businessmen were splashing out tens of millions of dollars to buy famous French Impressionist paintings, the museum's annual acquisition budget scarcely exceeded $1.5 million, hardly enough to buy more than one or two relatively minor works. Indeed, the Japan Culture Agency's total budget was not much more than $50 million, with which it runs seven museums in Tokyo, Osaka, Kyoto and Nara.

Of course, numerous smaller art museums are dotted around the capital with interesting collections. They were often founded by businessmen to display their private collections. One of the better ones is the Bridgestone Museum of Art near the Ginza. Long before the art-buying frenzy of the Bubble Era, Shojiro Ishibashi used his Bridgestone Tire fortune to collect French Impressionist paintings and modern, Western-style Japanese pictures. He later opened the museum in downtown Tokyo to display them. The relentlessly modern and newly renovated Hara Museum, located in the Shinagawa district, boasts about 600 contemporary pieces, including Americans Jackson Pollock, Robert Rauschenberg, and Roy Liechtenstein as well as Japanese moderns. They are all housed in the Bauhaus-style former residence of businessman Toshio Hara, who started the collection. The building was designed by Japanese architect Jin Watanabe, who also had a hand in the famous Nichigeki Theater, since torn down. It is one of a handful of 1930's era buildings left in the city, of which the most famous are the Dai Ichi Building of Douglas MacArthur fame (also by Watanabe) and the National Diet Building. In the Marunouchi district, with a spectacular view of the Imperial Palace grounds, not to mention some pretty spectacular works, is the Idemitsu Museum. It is funded by the Idemitsu Sosan, an oil refining company whose charter rather unusually cites exhibiting art as a corporate goal.

An exquisite little museum can be found just around the corner from the stock exchange. Taneji Yamazaki started out as a rice merchant and made a big fortune in the stock market. He plowed part of his money into art, becoming a major collector and patron of Meiji-era and post-Meiji Japanese paintings in the haunting *nihonga* style. When the company built its headquarters in 1963,

Yamazaki devoted two floors to a museum, The Yamatane Museum of Art, which he visualized as becoming a kind of oasis where brokers could take a quiet contemplative break from the frenzy of buying and selling just around the corner. The collection includes several pictures by 20th century masters, now designated "living treasures," such as Kokei Kobayashi and Guyokudo Kawai. Not on display, however, are any of the Western-style paintings that the Yamatane group purchased during the Bubble Era, as did so many other Japanese corporations. Indeed, it set up a separate division just to invest in foreign paintings. As Executive Vice-President Tadashige Nagasao explained, "If we buy a picture, it is treated as an asset, just like any other commodity on the bottom line." Yamatane, he said, held about 70-80 of these valuable "assets" in 1992, most of them Western-style paintings. There is no problem in storing them. One of the group's main businesses, in addition to stock brokering, freight-forwarding and rice milling, is warehousing.

The Bubble Era, of course, produced a bumper crop of new amateur collectors. Asahiro Takana, who made his fortune running taxi cabs, has amassed the world's largest collection of paintings by Marie Laurencins. Another serious new collector is Michimase Muraichi, who became a multi-millionaire by methodically selling his family's suburban rice paddies to Tokyo real estate developers. His collection boasts Corots and Courbets. Akira Mori, son of the late property developer and once world's richest man, is a well-known collector of Le Corbusier. Much of it is displayed at his ARK Hills Club, where membership is restricted to a select 1,000. Kusuke Nagashima, a pachinko magnate, has an eclectic collection of Picassos, Chagalls and Renoirs, while Ise Hikonobu, who made his pile selling eggs, has an extensive collection of Monets, Cezannes and Magrittes. Tokyo property tycoon, Shigeki Kameyama, made a big splash in the art world by paying $20 million to buy *Interchange* by Willem de Koonings, then the most money ever paid for a work by a living artist. He also laid out $2 million for Kenneth Nolan's *Empyrean*, confirming that the Japanese were willing to spend large sums for contemporary abstract works, not just French Impressionists. Yet not many are to be seen in Tokyo. Takana keeps his Laurencins in a distant mountain resort. The pinball magnate Nagashima displays his collection at a private exhibition hall in his hometown of Kagoshima in the far southwest.

There is considerable irony in this. People constantly complain that Tokyo is too big, that it is too concentrated, that it absorbs too much of the country's talent, while provincial towns wither and die. People talk incessantly about moving the capital somewhere else in the interest of decentralization. But in one arena, art, decentralization is a complete success. It sometimes seems as if every village big enough to have a gas station boasts its very own art museum. This trend was greatly accelerated during the 1990s as the Japanese government poured trillions of yen into public works projects to boost the economy in the post-Bubble economic recession. Smaller cities fastened on to art museums as one way of boosting the prestige of their hometowns. They hired famous architects to design splendid public galleries and bought expensive works to fill them. According to the Japan Association of Museums, more than 160 art museums existed by the end of the century, about half of them public facilities erected by cities and towns. Ibaraki prefecture, northeast of Tokyo, built a museum composed of ten pavilions designed by different international architects. The otherwise undistinguished provincial town of Mito, about an hour's train ride north of the capital, has in the Mito Art Tower, one of Japan's most innovative museums housed in one of the country's landmark new buildings. Its exhibits often surpass anything found in the capital.

At best, these are well-appointed places with ample budgets, professional curators and diversified and sometimes daring collections. At their worst, they barely qualify as museums. A rich businessman from the provinces buys one or two famous works and sets up a museum to glorify his name and his hometown, padding it out with inferior works. The tiny town of Onomachi in northern Fukushima prefecture, which has a population of only 13,000, spent so much money building its own culture center that it had precious little left over to buy any pictures. It stocked its walls with reproductions of works by Monet, Degas, Millet and Van Gogh. The town of Nagi, about a half-hour's drive from Tokyo, had a more creative solution. Rather than spend its small acquisition budget on mediocre works, it heeded the advice of architect Arata Isozaki, who designed the famous Mito Art Tower, and incorporated original art into the design itself, the three galleries becoming, in effect, the artwork.

The museum-building craze shows no signs of slowing down, even as economic hard times drag on. Japan would have 180 publicly funded art museums plus hundreds of private institutions by 2005. Some of these obviously make good sense. Nagasaki in southern Japan broke the trend of buying mostly French Impressionists and American moderns to specialize in contemporary Asian art. And who would begrudge Osaka, Japan's second city, its long-delayed Museum of Modern Art? But is there any reason why Fuchu, a generally non-descript bedroom community of 221,000 people in the Tokyo suburbs, should spend $55 million in public money on a new museum except for local civic pride run amok? It will concentrate on —- what else, Western-style paintings and modern Japanese artists. About 150 paintings have been purchased. Unusually, a local citizens group has been fighting the project, mostly unsuccessfully, because they find that it is grandiose and unsuitable for the size of the city. The recession has taken its toll on other institutions, however. A family feud threatened the Yamatane Museum, and financial circumstances forced Seibu department store to close its well-regarded Sezon Museum of Art.

If every little town can have its own art museum, Tokyo, naturally, could do no less, so the city fathers set out to build one. As far back as the early 1960s, they began quietly soliciting donations and making discreet purchases. In 1987, architect Takahiro Yanagisawa was commissioned to design a suitable structure. A reasonably generous acquisition budget of $75 million was appropriated, and Tokyo went on a worldwide shopping spree to top off its Japanese collection with famous Western works. The city's purchasing committee had assembled 480 major foreign works without attracting much attention — until in 1995 it splashed out $6 million on Roy Lichtenstein's *Girl with Hair Ribbon*, and caused a furor. It was hardly the most money ever spent by a Japanese public agency on a work of art. Osaka laid out $19 million on a Modigliani; Aichi Prefecture spent $17 million for *The Golden Knight* by Austrian painter Gustav Klimt; and, even rural Gunma prefecture spent $11 million for a Monet. But those purchases were made during the Bubble Era, when extravagance was the byword. In the more frugal era of Japan's post-Bubble recession, $6 million struck people as a lot of taxpayer money to dish out, especially for a "cartoon."

The Tokyo Museum of Contemporary Art is at one end of a public park in the middle of an unfashionable section of Koto Ward, east of the Sumida River. It is a strange location for an avant garde collection or for what is supposed to be one of the city's prestige projects, something that helps define Tokyo as a "world-class" city. One gets the impression that local politics entered the site's selection. It may have been a sop for Koto Ward authorities, who often feel put-upon because of the city's refusal or its inability to disperse refuse disposal more equitably. Koto Ward is famous as the gateway to the "Dream Islands," a euphemism for the garbage landfills on the edge of Tokyo Bay. This part of Tokyo was also decimated by the Great Kanto Earthquake, and much of the $430 million construction cost was spent on hardening the soil, pushing 222 special piers into the ground and other measures to keep it from collapsing. The permanent collection is housed in a heavy, gray granite, fortress-like structure that looks like it could indeed withstand a whole lot of shaking. But it does not appear to be heavily patronized. Only a handful of couples wander through the display rooms on a late weekday afternoon. Half a dozen rooms display paintings and sculpture. The Lichtenstein does not occupy any special place of honor; it is just one of half a dozen other works sharing wall space with an Andy Warhol self-portrait and a David Hockney. It isn't the MoMA, but it's a start.

In the small forest of skyscrapers west of Shinjuku Station is a curious Tokyo art museum. It is located on the 42nd floor of the Yasuda Fire and Marine Insurance Co., where the company maintains its own art museum. Much of the space is given over to a modern Japanese painter named Seiji Tojo. The walls are lined with his ghostly female figures in pale, pastel colors. At the end of one hall, however, in a separate room, are three paintings of an entirely different order. On the left side is a lovely painting of apples in a serving plate *Pommes et Serviette* by Paul Cezanne; on the right side, a warm autumn evocation of southern France, *L'Allee des Alyscamps* by Paul Gauguin. And in the middle is a striking array of spiky yellow blossoms set against a pale green background. It is *Sunflowers* by Vincent Van Gogh, one of the most famous paintings in the world. When Yasuda purchased *Sunflowers* at a London auction in March 1987, it was the first time that a work of art had sold for more than

£10 million. A lot more. Hajime Goto, company president at the time, said he felt it his duty to spend more than $39 million of his company's money so that the employees could enjoy great art and presumably participate vicariously in something a bit more exciting than selling insurance. The purchase set off an extraordinary scramble to buy famous (and not so famous) works of Western art that became one of the defining moments in Tokyo's modern history. Japanese collectors and corporations spent an estimated $8 billion on art in the four short years between 1987 and 1990. Indeed, it actually affected the country's balance of payments. During the latter part of the decade, Japan's overall trade surplus with the European Community declined, whereas it might have increased if the money spent on oil paintings had not been included. Art became Europe's second-most valuable export after automobiles. When in May, 1990, the late Ryoei Saito, then the retired chairman of the Daishowa Paper Manufacturing Co., spent $160 million to buy Van Gogh's *Portrait du Dr. Gachet* and Pierre-August Renior's *Au Moulin de la Galette* at a single auction in New York, it was the equivalent of buying a couple of Airbus jetliners. Under Japanese customs regulations the latter picture counted as a French import because it was painted in France, even though Saito bought the painting from a New York socialite, Mrs. John Hay Whitney.

Japanese collectors and gallery owners dominated the bidding at annual auctions held by Sotheby's and Christies' in London and New York. Sometimes as much as 40 percent of the lots sold went to Japanese bidders. Pretty soon Japanese collectors or museums were the proud owners of several versions of Monet's *Water Lillies*, Renoir's *Parisiennes in Algerian Costume*, Gauguin's *Two Breton Girls by the Sea*, Edouard Manet's *Self-Portrait* and Edgar Degas's *Woman Sponging Her Back*, among many others. "Nobody realizes how vast the Japanese market is," *The New York Times* quoted one London

Probably the closest thing to a Bubble Museum is the collection assembled by a Tokyo consumer loan company called Lake and is housed in a functional-looking warehouse in an older part of the capital near the Sumida River. None of the paintings is on public display, of course, and the receptionist would no doubt turn any casual visitor away politely. The paintings are kept in crates, except when they are taken out and put on a moveable board wall for certifiable buyers to inspect. Most of the paintings were acquired as collateral for loans during the height of the Bubble Era, and Lake set up a deal with Christie's to unload them in a series of auctions to be held between 1999-2003. Among the rumored treasures was the elusive *Pierrette's Wedding* by Picasso, which businessman Tomonori Tsurumaki bought in 1989 for more than $50 million, and which he hoped at one time to would be the masterpiece of a world-class art museum built around his Formula One motor race track on Kyushu. Then he was forced to yield it up to creditors. It is said that this seldom-seen Picasso keeps company with several thousand other much less distinguished works stored at the warehouse.

Slowly a number of paintings are beginning to emerge from Tokyo's art nether world. The tides of the art market are at full flow again, but this time running back in the direction of New York or London. New collectors with new riches have emerged to pick and choose from the rubble of the Bubble. Renoir's *Le Moulin de la Gallette*, which Saito purchased for $78 million was sold in 1998 to an undisclosed collector for $50 million and presumably left the country where it was never once put on display. Several other celebrated paintings will end their decade-long sojourn in Tokyo without ever once having seen sunlight, although a few museums have been able to intercept them for brief appearances. The Kawamura Memorial Museum of Art near Chiba, a suburb of

Tokyo, displayed eleven works by Anselm Keifer, which a credit union tycoon had purchased in the late 1980s for $13 million. The paintings were eventually seized by creditors, stored for years, and then unloaded on the Entwhistle Gallery in London for half the original price. But before they were whisked off to London, they were displayed for the first and last time in Japan at the Kawamura Museum. Some prefecture art museums have taken advantage of the depressed market to fill out their walls. Fukuoka spent $5.3 million to buy Salvador Dali's 1950 *The Madonna of Port Lligat*. Aomori Prefecture on the northern tip of Honshu, paid out $12 million to buy three Marc Chagalls, even though the museum won't open until 2003. These sales caused the *Nihon Keizai Shimbun*, Japan's leading financial daily, to scold public museum directors for using tax-payer money to relieve Japan's bad-debt problem by buying art from failed speculators.

Nautical images spring to mind as you walk into Tokyo's spanking-new International Forum. The curved glass atrium is docked on the edge of the Marunouchi financial district like some kind of glass *Titanic*. The effect is accentuated by the elevated walkways, looking like giant gantry ways, that connect the atrium with the performance halls. Inside, the structure is supported by steel columns placed at either end, holding up a lyrical array of curbed steel tension bars. Looking up at the roof feels for all the world like being inside the rib cage of a great blue whale. There is nothing else like the Forum in Tokyo — or anywhere else, for that matter. A combination of convention and exhibition center and a performing arts complex, it was the last and probably the most spectacular gesture of an era that has now faded into memory, except for the detritus of collapsing property prices, bad loans and economic stagnation. Planning began in 1986 on a site near the Marunouchi financial district, where the Tokyo city hall had been located. In 1991, the government offices moved into a towering complex in the Shinjuku district, which in itself is one of the most striking — and certainly controversial — buildings in the city.

The Forum was the object of the first international design contest in Japan to be officially recognized by the Union Internationale des Architectes, the Paris-based organization that is the world's most prestigious association of architects. The competition was won by Uruguayan-born New Yorker Rafael Vinoly, who had never before set foot in Tokyo. One can only admire Vinoly's ingenious solution to the puzzle created by a difficult location — a kind of trapezoid of space comprising about two city blocks, hemmed in on one side by the railway lines and on the other by the Marunouchi financial district.

The sweeping curve of the Glass Hall fits snugly against the wide band of rail lines. The other part of the complex comprises four performing halls, which are like Chinese boxes, each one slightly smaller than the other, seeming to fit inside one another. They echo the style of the nearby financial district, which is made up mainly of a succession of square, nondescript buildings. These two main elements of the Forum are separated by a landscaped outdoor plaza, a welcome stretch of greenery in the busy downtown area. Standing in the plaza and looking up at the massive facades of the buildings and the elevated walkways and escalators that connect them, the observer has a strange feeling of being indoors. And yet, at the same time, the bright sunlight streaming through the Glass Hall's massive, transparent walls, makes it feel like being outdoors. How do you keep 21,000 square meters of glass sparkling? Two cleaning robots are suspended from the end walls. At each segment, the robot extends four mechanical arms equipped with a rotating cleaning brush at the end. Each is capable of scrubbing about 300 square meters a day. It takes two months to cover an entire wall. The designers claim the Forum can survive an earthquake such as devastated Tokyo in 1923 or the one that hit the Kobe area in 1995. Yet, one would hate to be standing in the middle of the atrium, surrounded by all that glass, in the middle of a strong tremor.

The building has its critics, ranging from nit-pickers to those with more serious misgivings. The main convention hall accommodates more than 5,000 spectators, making it one of the largest in the world — but only by squeezing in so many seats that a rush-hour commuter train feels almost roomy by comparison. The upper loge, arching toward the rear ceiling like some kind of ski ramp, is so steep that you need a ski jumper's nerve to sit there. The distinguished architect Arata Isozaki is more sweeping in his condemnation. He describes the Forum as another "pile of garbage" on the Tokyo landscape. Isozaki is not particularly critical of the design itself, but of its dimensions. "It's wrong to erect a building of that size in that space," he says. The Glass Hall, 200 meters long and 60 meters tall, tends to overwhelm the individual, he complains. It is a monumental waste of space — a serious offense in a cramped city such as Tokyo.

The Forum is one more artistic legacy of the Bubble. The soaring value of the yen made it easy to hire the world's best architects in much the same way that corporations bought famous French and American paintings. The difference, of course, being that their works are fully on display, turning the capital into a kind of outdoor museum for the post-modern. Almost all the international stars — Norman Foster, Nigel Coates and Philippe Starck among them — as well as leading local talents such as Kisho Kurokawa and Maki Fumihiko have had a hand in remaking Tokyo. And they clearly didn't feel shackled by convention. Some of the new buildings, such as the new International Forum near the

Imperial Palace, are part of a civic-improvement scheme. Others simply represent the impulses of private companies. Over the past decade, the urban landscape has been punctuated here and there with arresting — and, in some cases, almost bizarre — buildings. Let us take a walking tour (metaphorically, since many of the buildings are widely separated from each other) of some of the capital's more interesting buildings. On the right side of Aoyama-dori street lies a building where everything looks askew. The windows on the Spiral Building, designed by Fumihiko Maki in 1985, cluster together in one corner, the rest of the surface is smooth except where it is occasionally broken by square holes. It has a playful look, as if it were made out of children's building blocks. Inside is a gallery with a wide, spiral staircase, which evidently gives the building its name, leading to the second floor. The space is usually filled with avant-garde art. The Spiral Building is owned by Wacoal, an old-line Kyoto brassiere company. It wasn't content simply to open a branch office. It wanted to make a statement. Its Tokyo headquarters in the Kojimachi district opposite the Imperial Palace is another of the city's more interesting new buildings. Designed by Kurokawa, it also has a playful look, with a curved canopy on the roof and a kind of bicycle chain gear effect on the side. Some say it looks like a sewing machine, an appropriate image, one supposes, for a lingerie maker.

But for sheer whim, nothing matches Philippe Starck's Asahi Super Dry Hall, built in 1989, in the Asakusa district. Where a huge, neon Asahi beer sign was once a beacon, there now looms what can only be described as an *objet*, a kind of golden beet resting on a black obsidian-like pedestal which doubles as a restaurant. This is the *Flamme d'Or*, or Flame of Gold, representing, we are told, the "burning heart of Asahi Beer." Or, maybe the head on a glass of that same product. Or, even a spermatozoon. Or, something from Ghostbusters. The flame is hollow; it serves no practical purpose. Call it architecture as sculpture. Typical of Tokyo, little thought has apparently been given to the setting. The Asahi torch is jarringly close to the Sensoji Temple, one of Tokyo's oldest and most traditional Buddhist sites. Much the same criticism can be leveled at the new Edo-Tokyo Museum (Kiyonori Kikutake 1992) built by the city to showcase its 500-year history. What this look-a-like of a Star Wars battle station has to do with Tokyo's past is a mystery. At any moment, you expect it to zap the graceful national sumo stadium next door and reduce it to galactic dust.

The overall impression conveyed by these buildings is one of rampant individualism. Very little thought seems to have been given to the setting or context. They are the maverick statements of individuals with fat pocket books and giant egos. Wrote *The Japan Times:* "Residents are proud of this city's architectural gems, but they also have good reason to regret the trickle-down influence on all the local would-be Kenzo Tanges, I.M. Peis and Norman Fosters who have crammed the streets with pretentious buildings while ignoring the most elementary notions of town planning or urban harmony. . . . The result is the typical Tokyo streetscape: rows of narrow, ill-matched buildings clad in pockmarked cement or patches of rusted metal or what look like leftover bathroom tiles, all competing for attention like so many paralyzed prima donnas." For those who recoil in shock at the sight of some of Tokyo's more outlandish architectural offerings, there is at least one consolation. Nothing lasts very long. Few buildings from pervious eras survived the twin disasters of the 20th century — the Great Kanto Earthquake and the carpet bombing of World War II. One day, no doubt, the legacy of the Bubble Era will disappear into the mists of history. All that will be left is Tokyo's dynamic eclecticism. And that is timeless.

## Sublime Kitsch

From Tokyo Station it is a short trip on the 'Romance Express' train to the lake and mountain pass retreat of Hakone, south of the capital. During the Edo Period, this was an important post station on the Tokaido Road, where Shogunate guards checked travelers to see if they were members of the noble families that were held hostage in Edo to maintain peace in the land. Today, it is a popular place to go for day-trips from the capital. In these mountains the Fuji Sankei Group operates an outdoor sculpture park called the Hakone Open Air Museum of Art. "In the midst of nature a space for man and art to meet, a museum symbolizing the essence of the Fuji Sankei Communications Group," says a sign at the entrance. Indeed, it is a beautiful place with many beautiful things in it.

On a late autumn day, as I wandered along the paths with other Sunday visitors and their children, the sky was bright and the nearby mountains russet-colored with dull red leaves of Japanese maple trees. The paths were lined with modern works by notable artists such as Alexander Calder, Kenneth Armitage and the English sculptor Henry Moore. Some of the latter, the display says, was donated by former U.S. Vice-President Nelson Rockefeller. As so

# 10

# Horizons

One night in March, several thousand workers began loading boxes into waiting trucks for a move across town. Tokyo's city government was moving its head offices from its old haunts in the Marunouchi district to a towering new city hall in Shinjuku (which, appropriately enough, literally means "new lodgings"). The move required 3,500 two-ton trucks — virtually every moving van in the city — to haul 260,000 container boxes filled with the files of 13,000 city workers, the governor, his four vice-governors and the members of the municipal assembly. When the move was completed three weeks later, one center of power in Tokyo had shifted in the most dramatic way from the downtown. Many with a traditional frame of mind were appalled at the move. After all, the heart and soul of Tokyo had, for generations, been concentrated around the palace and the low-lying flatlands to the east. Shinjuku wasn't even fully incorporated into Tokyo city limits until 1932, when the boundaries were expanded to make Tokyo once again the largest city in the world. Even today, Shinjuku is more a by-word for pleasure than for power.

Shinjuku Station and the lines of the various rail lines that converge there, however, form a kind of demarcation line between the pleasure quarters and department stores in east Shinjuku and the more austere and business-like west Shinjuku, known to everyone as Nishiguchi, or West Exit. It is here on the site of an old water purification plant that Tokyo's first cluster of sky-scrapers was built in the 1970s, giving a part of the city something of the feeling of downtown Manhattan. They were built there, in part, because the ground underneath Shinjuku is less prone to earthquake than other parts of the capital. Today, the West Exit boasts the headquarters of several large insurance companies, yet relatively few of the other giants of Japan's industry seem inclined to move there from the familiar home territory. It seems unlikely that the address Nishishinjuku will ever carry the same cachet as one in Marunouchi for some time to come.

Of the several new towers in west Shinjuku, the most imposing is Building No. 1 of the new Tokyo Metropolitan Government complex, the *To-Cho*, or city hall. Its huge facade juts aggressively upward. The whole impression is massive and imperial. In comparison, the National Diet Building looks almost puny. To many people, the faintly Gothic, battleship gray twin towers look vaguely like Notre Dame Cathedral. On the other hand, the regular pattern of lines and windows also suggests the criss-cross patterns of *rengoshi* sliding doors of traditional Japanese houses. Architect Kenzo Tange claimed he had a more modern image in mind. He said that the design was intended to be reminiscent of the layout and shape of a semi-conductor — the brain of a computer being an appropriate symbol for a world capital in the information age. Not everyone sees the allusion, but they agree that the building has the opening, eclipsing the record set by the Sunshine Building by four days. For those who were especially impressed, a Shinjuku department store offered a four-foot plastic model at 1/200 scale for ¥1.8 million. Other commercial tie-ins were also offered at the opening. Department stores stocked up on To-Cho rice cakes and whiskey. There was even a poet of the new building, one Manabu Tateyama, who wrote a book called **The Tokyo Metropolitan Government's Move to Shinjuku**.

But despite the thousands of tourists who visit daily and ride the elevator to the 48th floor to take in the view, Tokyo's new city hall seems unloved. Many find that its fortress-like proportions make it cold, bureaucratic and over-bearing. The billion-dollar city hall complex was widely derided as "tax towers" or sometimes "the tower of bubble," despite the governor's earnest insistence that no general tax money was used in its construction. The wherewithal, he said, came from special funds and the proceeds from the sale of city-owned properties. To many people, however, the new city hall complex seemed a perfect symbol of the overweening confidence of the Bubble Era and all of its excesses. The building opened just before the 1991 municipal election, and naturally it became an issue in the campaign. Much was made of the governor's plush seventh-floor office suite, including, it was said, a marble-lined shower stall. The incumbent found it politic not to move into his new office until after the election, while some of his opponents promised not to move in at all.

That same year, people flocked to the cinemas to see the latest version of the long-running series, *Godzilla vs. King Ghidora*. The emotional high point of the film comes when the rampaging reptile obliterates To-Cho, the new city hall building, usually accompanied by cheers from the audience. The model cost the studio about $700,000 to build. Despite its wacky plots, the

Godzilla series is often close to the pulse of public opinion. That version, for example, also addressed the then burning topic of American "Japan-bashing." Godzilla dispatches some American time-travelers, then he turns his attention on Tokyo's obsession with ostentatious displays of wealth by tearing down city hall. One could sense that Godzilla was acting out in a grand style the secret fantasy of every taxpayer. The beast has gone on to destroy other symbols of modern Tokyo. In the 19th epic, he flattens Yokohama's Landmark Tower, and in the 20th, he plows through Makuhari New Town.

The man who built the new city hall probably did more to transform Tokyo than any other individual since Ieyasu Tokugawa. Shunichi Suzuki served for 16 years (1979-1995) as governor. It says something about the stability and continuity of Tokyo's government that Suzuki could conceive the idea of a towering new city hall, commission its design, oversee construction and still be able to occupy it for a full four-year term. Between 1947, when the direct election was instituted, and the end of the century there have been only seven chief executives. And there were only four in the living memory of most Tokyoites. Probably the best loved was Ryokichi Minobe, who took office shortly after the 1964 Olympic Games, in 1967, and served three terms. A member of the Japan Socialist Party, he expanded social services, but throughout his tenure the city budget was almost always in the red. So when Minobe left office in 1979, Tokyo was in the middle of a financial crisis not unlike the one that nearly drove New York into bankruptcy in 1975. His successor, Suzuki, was an experienced administrator, a former high-ranking civil servant in the Home Ministry, and he immediately set about stopping the flow of red ink. He laid off city workers by the thousands, slashed his own salary in half, raised tuition at city schools, cut subsidies and instituted charges for municipal services that had previously been free. In two years, the budget was back in the black.

But Suzuki's real legacy was a grand new vision for Tokyo that he called "My Town Tokyo", his name for the technically sounding "Second Long-Range Development Plan for the Tokyo Metropolis". The plan promised to end "top-down" urban development that had alienated citizens. But the main thrust was really aimed at the needs of big business and the international community. He envisioned dispersing the city away from the expensive Marunouchi downtown to seven sub-centers, turning the city into a "multi-modal metropolis." He also spent heavily on building glamour projects to show off Tokyo as a "world city." All were conceived during Suzuki's long tenure, even if some of them were only completed after he left office.

Suzuki's Prestige Projects

| | | |
|---|---|---|
| 1. | Tokyo Metropolitan Gymnasium | 1990 |
| 2. | Tokyo Budokan | 1990 |
| 3. | Metropolitan Art Space | 1990 |
| 4. | Tokyo City Hall | 1991 |
| 5. | Edo-Tokyo Historical Museum | 1993 |
| 6. | Tokyo Museum of Photography | 1995 |
| 7. | Contemporary Museum of Art | 1995 |
| 8. | Tokyo (Big Sight) Exhibition Center | 1996 |
| 9. | Tokyo International Forum | 1997 |

By the end of the century, these nine projects alone were costing Tokyo taxpayers more than $200 million annually just to keep the lights on and the windows cleaned. Suzuki's vision for Tokyo has many critics, but it is, if nothing else, a plan. When he left office, Suzuki had put his stamp on his town in a way that is probably unequaled by any municipal leader since Robert Moses, the great mid-century builder of New York who was also much criticized.

Of the governor's many projects, the most ambitious by far was his proposal to build a huge futuristic "sub-city" on reclaimed land in Tokyo Bay. He called it "Tokyo Teleport Town" (for telecommunications port) to emphasize its future as a hub for information processing, computers being the cotton looms of the modern era. The governor conceived the idea for the ultimate planned community after attending a conference on "world teleports" in New York in 1984. He announced the project in 1986 and won the endorsement of then Prime Minister Yasuhiro Nakasone. Grand hotels, office towers, apartments, shopping arcades and cultural facilities would be constructed on 448 hectares of reclaimed land in Tokyo Bay. The development would require new bridges, tunnels and railroads to shuttle the salarymen and sightseers to the massive waterfront complex from the downtown, only six kilometers away. A state-of-the-art telecommunications center would be the showcase for Japanese technological achievements. Roughly 65,000 people would live there, and twice as many would commute for work each day. The estimated total cost: $100 billion. Nobody ever accused the governor of thinking small.

The project had a certain logic. Tokyo has always moved toward the waterfront when it needed more living space. It has been that way since Edo times. The first Tokugawa shogun had scarcely settled into his new capital in 1590 before he began digging moats and canals and dumping the soil in the marshy land next to the bulwarks of the castle. Much of what constitutes the modern-day Marunouchi and Yurakucho and the Ginza shopping district was once under water. The shogun ordered that the southern tip of Kanda Bluff be cut off, and the earth was dumped directly east of the castle, creating the land needed to build houses for craftsmen and merchants. The great fire of 1657 spurred another spasm of building. More of the harbor was filled in east of the Ginza in Tsukiji, which means "built-up land" in Japanese. Two mud flats at the entrance to the Sumida River were developed over time into a proper island, the long and narrow Tsukudajima. The Great Kanto Earthquake in 1923 provided plenty of rubble for island builders, as did the bombs in 1945. Land reclamation proceeded with a vengeance after the war, and it spread beyond the northwest corner near the city center to surround the entire bay. Much of the new land was used as platforms for factories, coastal highways and refuse dumps. Intent on rapid industrialization, the government allowed only energy, heavy industry and transportation companies to build there.

Waterfront development was one of the hottest investment themes during the Bubble Era. Declining smokestack industries such as steel plants or shipbuilding found their shares had new luster as investors looked beyond their decrepit yards and empty factories to the hectares of developable property along the shore. Construction stocks got a boost in anticipation of all the new bridges, subway lines, rail extensions and tunnels that would be needed. Stocks of companies with property along the water increased even if they professed no immediate plans to develop their land. When one brokerage company published a map showing various land holdings along Tokyo Bay, it became an instant bestseller. At one time, at least 40 major real-estate developments were planned around Tokyo Bay. The enormous inflation in land values in the city center made the shoreline seem like the only place left where new offices could be erected. Meanwhile, heavy industry was moving to cheaper locations in Southeast Asia or shutting down entirely. The bay was ringed with dozens of aging or abandoned shipyards, steel mills, railway marshaling yards or empty freight yards, all sitting on potentially lucrative real estate. For

Another "futuristic city of the 21st century" lies at the tip of Tokyo Bay. Technically part of Chiba Prefecture, Makuhari New Town was meant to add thousands more people to greater Tokyo. Historically, the bay's northern end had been neglected. Development spread southward from Tokyo down the coastline toward Yokohama and Kawasaki. Until only a few years ago, nothing much appeared along this stretch of coast except a village and a sandy beach. People used to come out in the spring to gather seashells and in the summer to swim at the beach. Today, Makuhari town itself is a collection of gray, granite mid-rise buildings arranged in a grid pattern and divided by straight, wide streets with long pedestrian overpasses. Several large hotels rise next to the convention center, although one wonders who stays in them. Surely it can't be Tokyo residents, since it is only a 30-minute train ride from Tokyo station along the new branch of the Keiyo line. Perhaps it hosts businessmen visiting the several corporate headquarters that have relocated here, or, just across the coastal expressway, tourists enjoying the beach which was carefully rebuilt by Chiba authorities with additional sand and pine trees.

The buildings are all formidably "intelligent," equipped with the latest in satellite and fiber optical communications, computer-aided temperature control, pneumatic garbage disposal and district heating. But there is a certain lifelessness that one often associates with modern airport complexes or "edge" cities. All of these futuristic bay-side projects seem devoid of people. The streets are empty most of the day. Perhaps it is the dearth of commercial life. Chiba planners hoped to attract up-market department stores to give their new town some ready-made prestige. A site next to the railway station was selected and mapped out for a huge shopping mall. But caught in the post-Bubble slump, many Tokyo stores, as well as Bloomingdales of New York, delayed their plans to move there. But in late 2000, Carrefour of France, the world's second-largest retailer after Wal-Mart, opened its first store in Japan in Makuhari, drawing hordes of bargain-seekers on opening day.

The new town's centerpiece and biggest draw is the huge Nippon Convention Center, known to everyone as the Makuhari Messe. *Messe* is German for trade fair. Architect Fumihiko Maki designed it to resemble a free-floating space station, no doubt a fitting symbol for a "futuristic city." The complex covers 17 hectares and houses three major exhibition rooms. The biggest event held there is usually the Tokyo Motor Show, where, every two years, Japan's automobile manufacturers show off their new designs in a spectacular exhibition that lasts for two weeks and draws crowds by the millions. The highlight of the motor show is always the "concept" cars, when Japan's automakers show off their cars of the future: electric powered, advanced aerodynamics, and stocked with intelligent equipment that helps the driver navigate without crashing. It is understood that few of these concept cars will ever make it into the showroom, but they do provide clues to the shape of things to come.

In much the same way, Japan's construction companies and their expensive architects came up with their own "concepts" for reshaping and redesigning the ever-changing capital. Like their counterparts at the auto show, most of these designs will never proceed beyond the stage of artist's renderings and models — and the post-Bubble recession forced many corporations to stick their grand plans back in the drawer and their models into storage. But once the warm winds of prosperity beginning blowing again, expect to see them taken out, brushed up, and possibly turned into concrete and steel transforming Tokyo once again out of all recognition: fantastic super skyscrapers so tall that air must be pumped into the upper stories so that the inhabits don't faint from oxygen deprivation; huge floating islands covering much of the bay; vast underground cities that never see daylight except such as filters down through elaborate skylights. Imagine returning to the Tokyo of, say, 2020. Dominating the skyline might be a needle-like stele of Norman Foster's Millennium Tower, which at 800 meters is about twice as tall as any other structure in the city, including Tokyo Tower (which by 2020 may have been dismantled rod by rod and moved to suburban Saitama prefecture.) More than a mere building, the Millennium Tower is a small township with a permanent population of 50,000 people, who travel back and forth from its location at the upper end of Tokyo Bay by high-speed ferries. But Foster's project is relatively modest compared with some of the other proposals that teased the world in the 1990s.

Skyscrapers that exceed 100 stories would have seemed unimaginable in Tokyo a few decades ago. Fear of having them tumble over in another big earthquake kept the skyline relentlessly low. The first structure that looked anything like a skyscraper was the Kasumigaseki Building, erected near the Imperial Palace in 1968. It is a mere 36 stories. Then came the cluster of mini-skyscrapers west of Shinjuku Station, all about 40 stories high. Since then, buildings have risen to about 50 stories or more, among them the Sunshine 60 Tower in Ikebukuro and City Hall. Tokyo's existing high-rise buildings are constructed so that they sway with the motion of an earthquake, like a weeping willow tree bending in the wind. This works well enough up to about 100 stories. But in taller buildings, the swaying would become so pronounced from ordinary wind, not to mention typhoons or earthquakes, that the residents on the upper floors could suffer from perpetual motion sickness. So new technologies are needed that allow buildings to essentially shift their weight to compensate for the sideways motion. Thus Kajima Corp.'s proposed 200-story Dynamic

Intelligence Building, or DIB-200, incorporates seismic sensors on the inside and outside to detect movement and vibrations. The data is collected and analyzed by computers that operate a system of controls that change the building's center of gravity to maintain its equilibrium. This would be done by transferring water from storage tanks located at strategic locations. Another problem is how to move people vertically the equivalent of several city blocks on an ordinary horizontal street front. The Landmark Tower in Yokohama, currently Japan's tallest building, already boasts the world's fastest elevators. It has 51 elevators, three of them shooting directly to the observation tower on the 69th floor in about 40 seconds. Taller buildings would have, in effect, sky trains that move upwards.

Virtually all of the proposed super skyscrapers are severely geometrical in shape, full of triangles, cones, cuneiforms, oblongs and cylinders. The intricately designed Taisei-100 starts out as an octagonal building, turns cylindrical, then box-like and finally cross-shaped. Kajima's DIB-200 rises to its tremendous height by stacking identical 40-story cylindrical modules, sixteen in all, next to and on top of each other to create a lattice effect. Such aerodynamic surfaces, of course, are designed to lessen the amount of surface that is directly exposed to wind and typhoons, but they also seem to be an expression of a Japan's love affair with geometric forms and symmetry. One can see this in many ordinary expressions of life, from the traditional tatami mats fitted together to form a pattern, to the extraordinary profusion of different shapes of tableware.

From the high city to the low city, the land under Tokyo offers yet more potential for reshaping the city. The people of Tokyo have a considerable life underground already. The subway system is one of the world's largest, and there are numerous underground

The subtext of almost all of these projects is that Tokyo is rapidly running out of usable or affordable space in which to provide a place to live for many more thousands of people drawn inevitably to the capital. Or, conversely, that something dramatic must be created to stem the inexorable tide of people moving further and further into the far suburbs. Hence, buildings that are really whole cities, that jut a kilometer into the sky, or spread out for miles underground. Thus, architects unveil plans to fill in or build over the northern reaches of the Tokyo Bay. Kisho Kurokawa's Project Noah envisions creating an entirely new city of about 5 million on about 30,000 hectares of artificial land. It would be 70-times larger than Tokyo Teleport town and take some 840 million cubic meters of land fill, obtained, he says, by dredging the lower approaches to the bay to a depth of about 20 meters and by digging huge looping canals around the city to act as fire breaks in the event of another great earthquake. He reckons about 2 million people would move out of the old city reducing population pressures and land prices and providing space for more woodlands. Another rather bizarre plan, envisions a second city built directly on top of the existing one. Imagine that one in a major earthquake! Yet, by any objective standard, Tokyo is far from over-built now. Despite some new high-rise additions, it remains basically a city of single-family dwellings and modest apartments. Certain new developments, such as Rivercity 21, a cluster of expensive high-rise residences near the mouth of the Sumida River get a surprising amount of attention if only because in Tokyo's context the idea of high-rise living is so unusual. Certainly in Hong Kong, for example, the complex would hardly merit a passing glance.

Anyway, none of these fantasy projects has received any kind of official approval, although there are government task forces in the ministries that are tackling the technical and regulatory problems associated with them. In fact, the Diet has already approved legislation that limits ownership of land to no more than 50 meters below ground. That enables the construction of new subways, highways — and possibly underground cities — without having to compensate the owners above. Already the new Shinjuku-Nerima subway line was built utilizing the benefits of this new law. Perhaps most of the bold visionary designs being dreamed up by Japanese architects are fated never to make it from drawing board to reality. But even if only a few are built, they could make Tokyo the most exciting and innovative urban laboratory of the 21st century.

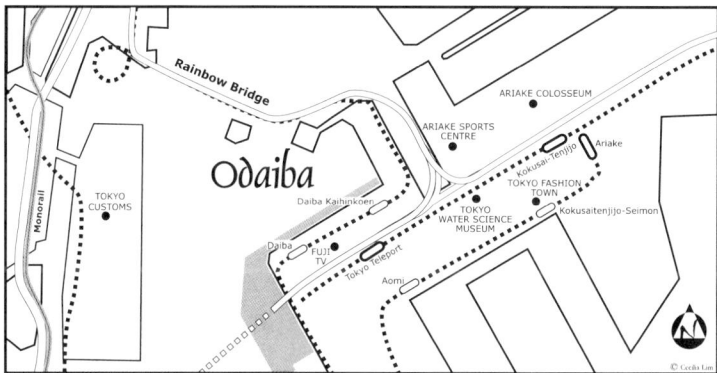

## On the Waterfront

A solitary ship makes its way under the bridge and lazily up the channel. Seagulls honk overhead. The silver wake of a ferry boat traces a path toward the new Hiruma passenger terminal with its arresting pyramidal dome. In the haze of the late afternoon, I can just make out the spire of Tokyo Tower and further to the right, fading into the horizon are the cluster of high-rise buildings in Shinjuku. I had joined a group of Japanese inspecting one of the capital's newest attractions, the Odaiba waterfront and the new Rainbow Bridge that connects it with the mainland.

An elevator bore us to the observation deck on the bridge's sixth deck and, as we walked out onto the span, the waterfront stretched before us. As we approached the end, two square green patches come into closer view. They are all that remains of the *daiba*, or coastal fortifications, that were hastily constructed after an American named Perry made a rude and uninvited appearance in Tokyo Bay in 1853. Beyond that stretches an expanse of flat land that used to be designated on maps, prosaically, as "No. 13 Reclaimed Land." Today it has a new name and an important new role in Tokyo's scheme of things.

The Odaiba waterfront was, of course, to have been the core of former Governor Shunichi Suzuki's grand plan for a futuristic center for international finance and commerce. In time, it may develop along those lines, but for the moment relatively few corporations have moved their headquarters onto the island. A prominent exception is the Fuji Television Network, perhaps the nation's most influential broadcaster. Its striking new glass and chrome building stands out on the waterfront, looking like it was built with an Erector set. Several other signature buildings have been erected, such as the modernistic Big Sight convention center with its distinctive dome looking like an inverted pyramid.

But Odaiba seems less some kind of futuristic city and more another kind of up-market amusement park with a few offices and apartments thrown in for good measure. One approaches the development on a computer-controlled monorail that circles the island. It has no driver, so the premium seat is at the front, offering a nice view of the waterfront. There is a "Frontierland" (the old forts), a Maritime Museum, shaped, naturally, like a ship, a "Tomorrowland" and Toyota's new "Palette Town" which boasts the

# 11

# Past

People rattle across the metal gangplank to board the water bus *My Town*. Even though it is a Friday, a working day, a large crowd is on board. School girls dressed in sailor uniforms wielding disposable cameras and older men and women with tour badges on their lapels make up a good part of the crowd. A mechanical voice comes out of a speaker in the ceiling and announces, "Welcome aboard, Ladies and Gentlemen," and a few moments later the motorized barge pulls away from Hinode Pier. As the boat gradually picks up speed, it passes the backside of the Tsukiji produce and fish market and heads towards the mouth of the Sumida River. It is only a forty-minute trip up the river to Asakusa, but, metaphorically, it is an expedition into another time.

Any boat trip up the Sumida today must be a mental excursion to a large degree. It takes a leap of imagination to find anything very interesting in the concrete flood embankments and automobile expressways that virtually line its entire length. The eight meter-tall flood walls block the view of the river for anyone who might want to stroll along its banks, assuming that a footpath were there to walk on. One can hardly argue with their utility. Floods have been almost as disastrous in this part of the city as earthquakes and fire. But only rarely does one catch a glimpse of the black tile roof of what might be an elegant restaurant peeking out over the top of the floodwalls. For the rest, it is mostly a dreary jumble of gray or ochre-colored warehouses and the backsides of apartment buildings.

The water bus takes a slight turn as it passes by Tsukishima island near the river's mouth. Fishermen living on this island in early Edo days cast their nets at night to catch ice fish swimming down the Sumida. The Shogun found them especially tasty, and a consignment always went to the castle. Messages were also dispatched to the castle, since the fishermen of Tsukishima were also employed to keep a look out and report on any suspicious movements in the upper reaches of the bay. Some enclaves on the island still retain some of the flavor of the old city, especially one called Tsukuda, named after a village near Osaka where the fishermen originally came from. One approaches this neighborhood across a handsome bridge tipped with bright red wooden posts. Canal skiffs are still moored in a tiny harbor. It's hard to say whether many people living here still make a livelihood from the water. One doubts it, but a visitor can still get a strong whiff of the pungent concoction made of fish, vegetables and the soy sauce called *tsukudani*, which was invented and is still sold here.

Several old-style Japanese black-tiled houses dating from before World War II line one side of the street. On the window ledges are well-tended bonsai. Huge ceramic vats, originally placed there to hold water to extinguish fires, have been turned into giant planters or tanks for goldfish. These and the colorful little harbor tend to attract artists on fine days. Five of them were busy sketching the scene in black ink on that Friday afternoon. Wherever there is something picturesque left in Tokyo, one often encounters artists with their sketchpads and paint kits. It is as if they feel they must get it on canvas before it all disappears. Across a canal rise the three towers of the River City 21 high-rise apartment complex. "An area that symbolizes the future of Tokyo," intones the mechanical voice from the ceiling of the water bus.

The water bus passes under the first of thirteen major bridges that span the river. There were no bridges across the Sumida River in early Edo. The Shogun appreciated that the river formed a natural defensive barrier on the east side of his new capital. After the disastrous fire of 1657, which razed the teeming craftsmen's and merchant's districts, the city administrators recognized the value of spreading the growing population of the city across the river. But even by Meiji times in the late 19th century, only a handful of spans existed. The scarcity of bridges, and their vulnerability to fire, caused many deaths during the great earthquake. Now there are more than a dozen bridges and it seems like one is continually passing underneath one as the motor boat makes its way to Asukusa, each bridge painted a different color for easy recognition.

Some of the bridges are famous. Probably woodblock print artist Hiroshige's most famous image, out of the thousands that he produced, is the sudden rain storm breaking over the Shin Ohashi Bridge, across the Sumida River. Looking at the picture today one can almost hear the thunderclap as the people on the bridge scatter in opposite directions. There is still a Shin Ohashi bridge at this location today, although it is made of concrete and iron and crowded with cars and pedestrians. The first bridge, built in 1647, was simply the Ohashi or Great Bridge. The next one became Shin Ohashi, or New Great Bridge. Shin Ohashi has kept its name but the first one is now called the Ryogoku.

Perhaps the most majestic is the Kiyosu Bridge. Completed in 1928, it is modeled on a suspension bridge in Cologne, Germany, with graceful arches and steel girders. The earliest and probably the most celebrated of the Sumida River spans is the Ryogoku Bridge. The Ryogoku figures in countless woodblock prints of the Edo period, often with bursts of fireworks against the skyline. Bustling crowds of people swarm around either end in makeshift market stalls, tea houses, and archery galleries, the entrances to bridges then being the main public spaces, the piazzas of the Shogun's city. Hiroshige himself described the Ryogoku Bridge as "the liveliest place in the Eastern Capital." Today it is difficult to recreate, even in imagination, the same atmosphere of pleasure around the Sumida River's bridges.

Edo was a city built on water, something that may be hard to visualize today. After all, many of the canals that used to criss-cross Edo, making it a kind of Venice of the East, were filled in during periods of rapid economic growth and others languish in permanent shadows of elevated expressways. Looking at the 19th century pictures today, it is amazing how important water, either as rivers, canals or shoreline, was to the daily life of Edo. When Hiroshige designed his celebrated series of woodblock prints called *One Hundred Famous Views of Edo*, the Sumida River and its shoreline figured prominently in about a quarter of them. Yet some parts of the old city along the Sumida still retain something of that watery feeling.

Entering the river proper, the boat passes a neighborhood called Fukagawa. This district was the epitome of the vital, plebeian quarter of the city that Edo people called the *shitamachi*, or low city, to distinguish it from the "high city" to the west where all the feudal lords, their samurai and retainers had their estates. The Fukagawa neighborhood was a warren of wooden houses, rice merchants and timber dealers. The latter did a roaring business as this and other parts of the city burned down regularly. One of the most successful timber merchants of his day, Bunzaemon Kinokuniya, left a large estate in this area, which eventually passed into the hands of the founder of the Mitsubishi business empire. He turned it into an exquisite garden, importing beautiful rocks from all over Japan. Today Kiyosumi Garden is a public park with a large lake filled with carp as its centerpiece.

Nearby is the Fukagawa-Edo Museum, run by the Koto Ward authorities to show what one neighborhood might have looked like about 30 years before Commodore Perry entered the bay in 1853 and changed Japan forever. The museum is filled with life-size buildings where you can walk in, take your shoes off and pad about on the tatami touching the furniture and the utensils. On one side is the stately shop-home of a rice merchant, the black tile roof denoting that he was a person of means. Over there a vegetable shop and a boatman's tavern. Everything is reconstructed with great attention to detail, even humor. A dog, frozen in time, lifts his leg against the post of a fire wooden watch tower. A cat dozes on the black-tile roof of a building. The lighting and sounds change to suggest the atmosphere of the neighborhood at different times of day. A rooster cackles at dawn followed by the piercing chants of the street vendors. A temple bell signals six o'clock in the evening as an orange sunset colors the canal by the museum's wall.

Something of the mood of the place lingers as one walks back towards the river. Echoes of old Edo resound on the streets of the modern town. In one shop-home, a craftsman sews the ends of tatami. Next door in the rice shop, different grades are now neatly stacked in plastic bags rather than in wooden tubs. The liquor store still displays *sake* in wooden barrels in the store window even though it also stocks a range of French cognac and Scottish whiskey inside. Of course, there were also video rental stores, too, and every once in a while there is a gap, which these days always seems to be filled by those ubiquitous doubled-tiered parking contraptions.

Next to one of the canals is a factory, probably some kind of tube manufacturer, which looks like it, too, belonged in some kind of museum of the manufacturing age. It is a reminder that this part of Tokyo was a cradle of Japan's industrial revolution. The famous Ishikawajima shipyards were built near the mouth of the Sumida in early Meiji times, and before World War II the area was dotted with small and large factories in a bewildering variety. Meiji-era maps show this area dotted with belching smoke stacks. While most of the larger factories have moved away, hundreds of smaller manufacturing enterprises and cottage industries are still scattered throughout the Sumida Ward. They average between four to seven workers, and two-thirds of them are family-run. Some of them are basically crafts shops, making such things as battledores, paddles used in the colorful shuttlecock game that children play at New Years. Most of the others are more traditional manufacturers, producing all kinds of metal accessories, glassware or *tabi*, socks with a separate pocket for the big toe. The Sumida Ward authorities, who were eager enough to see the large, polluting industries move somewhere else, now actively encourage small industries, and a few of them have established display halls where visitors are allowed to wander in and watch what is going on.

By the 1960s and 1970s, the Sumida River had become a cesspool. The fish disappeared, swimmers moved to public pools and pleasure boats vanished. But by most standards, the Sumida is living and breathing again and cleaner now than it has been in decades. One can again see the *yakata-bune,* or gondola-like pleasure boats, moored along the sides or in the connecting canals. The newspapers report that about 200 of them are back on the exposing in lengthy detail the complex series of deals by which the two paintings, which probably entered Japan sometime in the mid-1980s, passed through the hands of various dealers at ever increasing prices, eventually to be purchased by the Mitsubishi Corp. They finally landed in a collection put together by the immensely rich Soka Gakkai, the lay organization of the Nichirin Buddhist sect which is now one of the largest religions in Japan. The sect owns an art museum in Hachioji, which is so far out in the western suburbs of Tokyo that it is practically in the countryside. A twenty-minute taxi ride from the railroad station, past rice paddies and farm houses, deposits the rider at their Tokyo Fuji Art Museum, another of those small art museums that seem to be located in the most unlikely places. It had by decade's end acquired an the usual requisite collection of Western paintings by Manet, Utrillo, Sisley and, unusually for Japan, several Dutch Renaissance works. Conspicuously missing were the two Renoirs that were supposed to be the museum's centerpieces. The owners were evidently too embarrassed by all the bad publicity to put them on display.

Suppose all of the paintings that the Japanese acquired during that extraordinary four-year period could be assembled and displayed in one venue. Call it the "Museum of Bubble Art". Would it compare in stature with some of the other great art museums of the world? The question was put to Susumu Yamamoto, the dapper director of the Fuji Television Gallery and one of the more discriminating dealers in Japan. He scoffed at the idea. "No," he replied. "On the one hand, it would be too eclectic. On the other hand, only about one percent of it would be worth displaying. I'd say about 80 percent of it is junk, or at least very hard to resell. Just because one has big buying power, doesn't mean you have discrimination. They [the buyers] weren't collecting; they were just speculating."

hallmarks of the Tange style: enormous mass and fortress-like solidity. Inside, the visitor is overwhelmed with gray. The Tokyo government, which conducts public opinion surveys on every imaginable topic, once asked residents, "What is the color of Tokyo?" About half of the respondents said, "Gray". In stark contrast to the rich brocade furnishings of the national parliament, the chamber where the Assembly meets is spartan.

There are three buildings in the complex, home for about 18,000 municipal workers, who had the usual grumbles that people have when they move into brand new quarters. The elevators did not work properly, and attempts to brighten the workspaces were frustrated by authorities who banned individual flower pots and portable coffee-tea makers for fear that spilled water might seep under the carpets and short out the wires for inter-office communication in this the smartest of intelligent buildings. Later, they brought in about 1,000 big potted plants to soften the contours. When the new complex first opened, many wondered whether the influx of thousands of new workers would overwhelm the capacity of the noodle shops and restaurants of west Shinjuku, there being cafeteria space for only about 2,000 at a time. Many officer workers bring their own box lunches and on sunny days eat in the spacious courtyard, where, if they are so inclined, they can look at some 38 pieces of original sculpture that surround the semicircular "citizen's plaza."

Until the completion of Yokohama's Landmark Tower, Tokyo city hall was at 48 stories the tallest building in Japan. To the annoyance of the owners of the Sunshine Building in Ikebukuro, previously the capital's tallest structure, people flocked to the building to see the splendid view from the comfortable observation level. It was duly recorded that Tokyo city hall received its one-millionth visitor, a six-year-old girl, only 104 days after the shopping malls linked with them. One can walk from Hibiya Park near the palace almost to the waterfront, a distance of two kilometers, through the underground concourses of the several subway lines that converge near the Ginza. There are exits along the way if one feels a urge to come up for sunlight. The Otemachi subway station in the financial district sprawls over 41,000 square meters. It seems like one walks forever along colorless concrete corridors, looking for the right subway platform or any of the 59 exits that lead back to the street level. One is therefore relieved to find in one corner a tiny artificial garden, looking like an oasis of color in the drab surroundings. It is a small space carpeted with fake turf and surrounded with live potted bamboo, pine and ferns. Within the space is a small red lacquer bridge crossing an irregularly shaped pond stocked with about ten rather large living goldfish. It also includes a few decorative rocks and a bench. "We've made this space for your use. Use it as a place to meet people. We'll be pleased if you use it — Otemachi Station staff."

But underground subways and shopping malls are one thing, whole cities beneath the ground are another. Taisei Corp.'s "Alice City" project, named after Lewis Carroll's fantasy, envisions huge concrete cylinders buried as much as 150 meters below ground. Each module is large enough to accommodate offices, hotels, theaters and a life support system for a subterranean population of 100,000. A young team of designers at Shimizu Corp. has proposed an even grander plan, called Urban Geo Grid. Wide, cylindrical pods would be planted at even intervals under Tokyo. The only terrestrial evidence of their presence would be pyramidal glass atriums poking up from below the ground to gather sunlight for the offices, hotels and homes below. Subterranean tubes would link the "grid points", and, eventually, they would encompass an underground city of about 500,000.

water after disappearing for many years. They harken back to a time when the Sumida was the city's main traffic artery, and people took boats to admire cherry blossoms along the shore at Mukojima or to visit the government-licensed pleasure district at Yoshiwara, now long closed. These new yakata-bune are fitted out with tatami floors and enclosed with shoji screens. The glow from their red lanterns flickers on the water at night. Many young people have taken to renting them for summer parties, enjoying a dinner of sashimi and tempura. The fireworks display in late July, which had also been discontinued for many years, has been revived, although its location has moved upriver to near Asakusa from its traditional location near the Ryogoku Bridge.

Only two old restaurants, their black-tiled roofs peeking out from above the floodwalls, remain of what used to be one of the great pleasure centers of Tokyo. Yanagibashi on the west side of the Sumida was once a warren of expensive restaurants and lantern-lit streets. Customers would dine and enjoy a view of the river. In the early part of the century, Yanagibashi became one of the city's main geisha quarters. Almost nothing of this is left today. Concrete embankments cut off the view, and now the district is mostly an ugly jumble of warehouses and nondescript office buildings, virtually indistinguishable from the other districts that line the Sumida along this stretch. The Tokyo Metropolitan Government has developed an elaborate plan for the Sumida River, just as it has for every other part of Tokyo. This one envisions dividing the river district into three distinct areas. An international zone would be near the mouth, linking the Sumida with new office complexes. Further upstream would be a cultural zone centered on the historic Ryogoku and Asakusa, trying to integrate the charm of the old shitamachi with such modern buildings as the new Asahi Beer Garden and the national sumo stadium. The area furthest up river drew a picture of the Sumida with the drum tower dominating the foreground. It is a scene that could be imagined today if one managed to blot out the apartment buildings and expressways. For many years, the tournaments were held in the open air in the Ekoin Temple just south of the present stadium. In 1919, a proper stadium was built near the railroad station. After the war, it moved to temporary quarters on the other side of the river, but in 1985 it was back at what some might say was the proper side of the river in a modern, new Kokugikan.

The water boat turns towards the dock at Asakusa. The brief journey is almost over. The boat gently bumps against the dock, the motor shudders. Passengers waste no time getting off. The trip has come to an end. "Please watch your step as you depart," says the mechanical voice.

is to be turned into a mix of commercial buildings and residences. Best of all, the ugly flood embankments would be replaced by stepped terraces with landscaping on them. The goal is to replace the retaining walls along the length of the river in 50 years.

Near the edge of the Sumida district is a hall dedicated to the memory of Japan's master of the *haiku*, Matsuo Basho (1644-1694), who lived near the water's edge in this part of Edo for some years before setting off on journeys that he celebrated in travel pieces and poetry. The museum is not very accessible for those who do not read Japanese, but it contains some interesting exhibits, including the poet's walking stick and cape, or at least facsimiles of them, and some haiku written in his own hand. Outside, the view of the river is blocked by the floodwalls, as usual. And from the vantage point of the water boat, the roof of the building is barely visible. Even so, the mechanical guide informs passengers that they are passing "the home of the famous poet Basho on the right." How many of the passengers tossing a glance in that direction, could make out the roof of the memorial hall from the apartment building on the left or the paper warehouse on the right?

As the boat passes beneath the Ryogoku Bridge, one can just make out the green-tiled roof of the national sumo stadium. It peeps through the maze of apartment buildings and expressways. On some days the wooden drum tower sports two white flags, the traditional announcement that a tournament is in progress. The rhythmic beating of the drums summons the fans to the match. They seem a bit superfluous in these days of mass communication, but they add to the atmosphere. Most tournaments are sold out for months in advance. Sumo is nothing if not traditional. The sport has deep roots in this part of Tokyo. By the early 19th century, a regular pattern of annual *basho*, or tournaments, was firmly established. In his celebrated woodblock print series, Hiroshige dealer after Saito made his big splash. "Maybe not, but we begin to get the picture, when a hitherto unknown Tokyo (sic) businessman spends $160 million on two paintings in a total of eight minutes."

Saito caused another furor when newspapers reported that he wanted to have the paintings cremated with him after he died. Irate editorials appeared in *Le Figaro* and the *Daily Telegraph*, and Saito soon recanted after seeing how his words had been interpreted literally in the Western press. His casual remark had been misunderstood as it passed through the cultural filter, he claimed. What he meant to say was that if you really love something, you naturally want to keep it when you died. He had no real intention of burning the pictures, he said. Perish the thought. Still, the episode raised disturbing questions: were the Japanese really to be trusted with some of the world's greatest paintings? Saito, in fact, was an experienced and discriminating collector, but others among Japan's nouveau riche bought masterpieces practically on a whim, or as a tax dodge, or a subtle bribe for a politician. The paintings, fortunately, survived Saito's death in 1996, but that doesn't mean that they were hanging on a wall somewhere. In Tokyo, paintings are not so much displayed as they are warehoused. One is left to wonder whether Saito ever got much joy from them, aside from the sheer pleasure of ownership. Supposedly, he considered donating them to some museum, or he may have aspired, like other Japanese collectors, to make them the centerpiece of a personal museum gracing his home town of Shizuoka. Beset with financial problems, he never got around to it.

By the end of 1990, it was over. The art market collapsed like so many tulips in the famous tulip bubble of 17th century Holland. The stock market crash of that year had made the country's wealthy feel considerably poorer. Japanese became scarcer at art auctions, or they sat on their bidding paddles. Auctioneers found lots going unsold or failing to reach their reserve prices. Picasso's *Still Life Under a Lamp* stayed in New York, instead of gracing the office of some Japanese managing director. Sales at Sotheby's slid from $1.6 billion in 1990 to $406 million the following year. At the fourth annual Shinwa art auction held in Tokyo in September 1991, only about 30 percent of the offered works were sold, compared with 80 percent the year before. Department store art galleries reported that their sales were down, and many galleries in Ginza teetered on the brink of bankruptcy.

Yet the Japanese had spent all of that money. What did they have to show for it? Nothing much. Few of the pictures were ever put on display — Yasuda's *Sunflowers* is a notable exception. One hears of people stumbling across famous paintings hanging in golf course clubhouses, restaurants, corporate lobbies, but many purchasers have been so secretive about their collections that even museum directors and other specialists don't know exactly where to find all of them. European art specialists trying to put together catalogues of French Impressionists or works of other styles in Tokyo, or sometimes even trying to track down the location and status of a single work, go home frustrated. It seems as if all the art disappeared into some kind of black hole. "I rarely see them except on those rare occasions when they appear in galleries or are offered for sale." said the Director of the Bridgestone Museum, Nobuo Abe. In 1994, the Bridgestone was able to put on an exhibition of 75 paintings by the French painter Claude Monet, a favorite of the Japanese. About 40 were from Japanese museums or private collectors. But some experts reckon that there are as many as 200 Monets in Japan, but it is only a guess.

Two other paintings that seemed to symbolize all of the shenanigans of the Bubble Era were by Renoir: *A Reading Woman* and *After the Bath*. The press dubbed them the "Mitsubishi Renoirs", after often is the case in Japan, this museum is a strange mixture of the exquisite and kitsch. Not far from the garden of Moore statues is a rather grotesque arrangement of fake Michaelangelo statues. It makes the museum look sort of like a Japanese version of Forest Lawn.

All paths eventually lead to the Picasso Pavilion. You can't miss it. It is the building with the single word "Picasso" bannered in 20-foot letters across the front. Fuji boasts that this was the world's first private museum dedicated entirely to the Spanish artist. The brochure says there are more than 230 works in the collection. But most of them seem to be drawings or examples of his exuberant and garish ceramics. Very few paintings were on display when I visited. Yet it is undeniably a big draw. The average visitor may not be able to tell Emilio Greco (the sculptor) from El Greco (the painter), but he has certainly heard of Picasso. The museum shop is crammed with Picasso memorabilia: Picasso ashtrays, Picasso scarves, and Picasso neckties. The Nikkei Group, famous for its stock market index, once asked 60 private collectors in Japan which painter they would like to buy most. At the top of everybody's list was Picasso. Of course, that isn't a bad choice by any means. Most art historians would agree that Picasso was perhaps the greatest painter of the 20th Century. But he is also a brand name, like Gucci, and the Japanese feel safe buying and admiring his works.

The Hakone Open Air Museum tells a lot about Japanese people's real attitudes toward art. The capital is dotted with art museums, but how many people are really interested in art? They will turn out in large numbers to see famous works of European artists, especially if they are French masters. Japan opened its doors to the West in 1868, just as the French Impressionist movement in painting was getting underway. It made, forgive the word, a big impression. Even today, French paintings are held up in schools as the epitome of Western art. It was also a time when the art currents of Japan and Europe came together and mingled in mutual creativity. Early visitors to Japan were charmed by woodblock prints and sent them back home in large numbers. At the time, the Japanese were not so impressed, considering them a relatively low form of commercial art. Many European artists, Van Gogh among them, saw the prints, incorporated Japanese techniques into their own work and openly acknowledged it.

Exhibitions of famous European works have a long history in Japan. Both the *Mona Lisa* and *Venus de Milo* have made the tour. Almost every time I am in Tokyo, it seems like a major exhibition of some important Western artist is going on. The "Portraits of the Louvre" exhibit at the National Museum of Western Art in Ueno, in 1991, attracted 470,000 visitors. Long lines stretched well around the building as people waited patiently to get in. You had to elbow your way through the crowds to get close enough to look at the pictures.

In early 1999, France dispatched one its most celebrated works, Eugene Delacroix's *La Liberte Guidant le Peuple*, a vast canvas portraying the famous barricade during Paris's three-day revolt in 1830, "La Liberte" herself holding high the French tri-color flag. It arrived in Japan with great fanfare aboard an Airbus Beluga, the world's largest civilian cargo jet, no doubt providing a plug for the French commercial jetliner industry. Then it was put on display in a special room at the National Museum of Art. Also loaned was a smaller version of another well-known piece of Franco-American sculpture — the Statue of Liberty. Rather than the outdoor museum in Hakone, however, it graced the boardwalk of Tokyo's new Odaiba waterfront, where young couples came and had their pictures taken standing in front of it.

— T.C.

architects, construction companies and urban planners this was a golden opportunity to turn their futuristic visions into reality. Dream towns would rise where once there were only abandoned warehouses, old-style piers and deserted factories.

But the most ambitious of the new waterfront projects is Suzuki's futuristic new city. It is to be the ultimate urban commercial development, grander than London's Canary Wharf or New York's Battery Park. There were compelling reasons to build on this island. The most obvious were the 448 hectares of flat, undeveloped land that was totally owned by the metropolitan government, potentially only ten minutes from the Ginza district by rail. Here the government could plan and build a new city unencumbered by the enormous complexities, not to mention the extraordinary expense, of having to buy out hundreds of small landowners. Best of all, the trillions of yen needed for the entire project, including bridges, the subway lines sewage and garbage disposal facilities, could be financed through rents and key money (deposits) charged to the blue-chip companies that city officials were confident would flock to this new city on the bay.

The rosy vision of a new urban subcenter faltered when land prices began falling at the end of the Bubble Era. Land prices in the city, ostensibly one of the reasons for moving toward the waterfront, fell inexorably in the ensuing months and offices remained vacant. Desperate to attract tenants, the municipal government began to scale down rents, first by 17 percent and then by 40 percent. At one time these officials had hoped to finance the cost of this multi-billion dollar project entirely through rents and key money. Now they had to sell billions worth of bonds to finance all of those roads, bridges, tunnels and railway lines that were essential if this futuristic city were to have a future. "It is by no means unusual to cover the costs of such things as new roads and sewers through public financing," explained Suzuki's waterfront point-man then Vice-Governor Shunryu Takahashi. Not unusual, perhaps, but not popular either, especially if it is perceived that all of that taxpayer money was going mainly to benefit a few large corporations or to satisfy the megalomania, as some argued, of Governor Suzuki.

The governor had wanted to cap his career by hosting a world's fair on the bay, the Urban Frontier Exposition, in 1994, the last year of his term. Why not? Robert Moses had crowned his life's work with a fair in 1964. Baron Georges Eugene Haussmann celebrated the Universal Exposition in 1867 after remaking Paris. Suzuki could do no less. It would have been a fitting end to his career as well as serving as a spectacular advertisement for the governor's pet project. But corporate sponsors and foreign exhibitors were slow in coming. Other delays meant that the planned Expo had to be postponed until 1996, after the governor would leave office. It also made sure that it would become an issue in the 1995 municipal election. Suzuki tried to pass his office to what some have called his bureaucratic clone, one Nobuo Ishihara, a high-ranking civil servant in the home ministry. Ishihara garnered the support of every political party in the city except the communists. But by then the city's voters had grown tired of insiders and their grandiose plans. In a massive rebellion, they spurned the gray candidate for somebody they thought had a little more pizzazz. He was a former television personality best known as "pesky Grandma", a 1970s television character who cross-dresses, turned politician named Yukio Aoshima. Running as an independent, he spent nothing on his campaign except his filing fee. While the other candidates' sound trucks trolled the streets, he stayed at home supposedly studying books on city administration. And he promised to cancel the world's fair, which he promptly did after winning office in a landslide.

world's tallest ferris wheel. In short, the Odaiba waterfront is another Disneyland, or maybe a Coney Island.

Palette Town is basically a soft sell for the Toyota Corp. Two huge floors have been turned into a kind of showroom, and for a small price one can choose from a dozen or so models to take out for a short test ride. I tried another attraction called the "EcomRide" which allowed me to experience a "futuristic short-range transit system." I climbed into the little car, strapped on my seatbelt, punched in my "destination" on the control panel and settled back as the car trundled along at about 10 km per hour. Sometimes it even accelerated to a head-spinning 15 km/h. It traveled along a kind of roadway through the showroom until it came to a rather abrupt stop and I was ushered out. Not the most exciting of rides.

A lot of people who go to the Odaiba waterfront are young couples. It has become a fashionable date spot, maybe THE date spot in the capital. By day, you can see them strolling hand-in-hand along the artificial beach, watching the wind surfers or ambling along the boardwalk of the Tokyo Decks mall. They sample New York Brownies and bagels or triple-decked ice cream cones topped with jellybeans. On warm summer evenings, they can sit on benches and snuggle and look across the water at the colorful lights that festoon the Rainbow Bridge and, beyond that, the city itself. If they are in the mood and have the means to pay, they might repair to the privacy of Odaiba's two large luxury hotels.

What is obviously lacking in Odaiba, indeed in any of these "futuristic" waterfront cities, are ramen noodle shops, public baths, narrow alleyways or anything else that would remind anyone that he or she lives in Japan. Also hard to find are convenience stores, bank outlets, laundries or the other mundane but necessary attributes of normal neighborhood life. While the boardwalk is often full of people, the rest of Odaiba and the waterfront seem empty and sterile. It lacks a street life, indeed it lacks streets save for expressways. "I wouldn't want to live here," said one of my Tokyo friends as we traveled along on the monorail. Odaiba is pretty spectacular, but it will take a long time until people really feel comfortable living there.

— T.C.

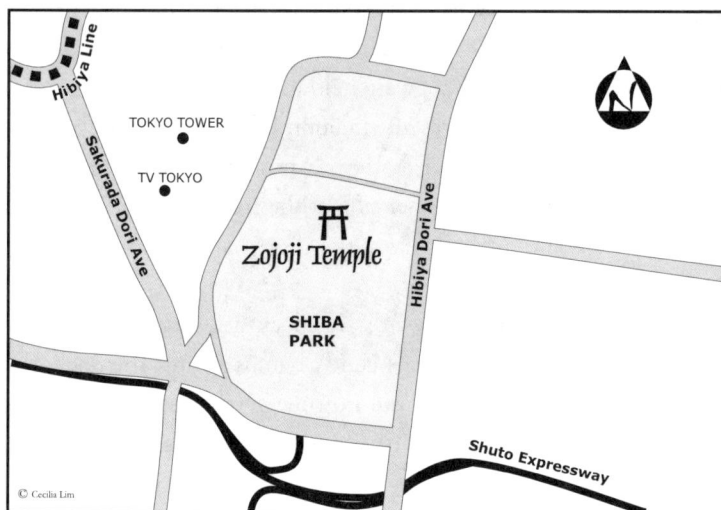

© Cecilia Lim

*Impermanence Forever*

With Tokyo Tower looming in the background, a golf driving range covered with an enormous green net off to the right and two bowling alleys closing in, Zojo-ji Temple seems to get no respect. Once it was the main temple of the Tokugawa clan, rulers of Japan from 1603 to 1868. Today it is just another temple, albeit larger than most in Tokyo and in a more affluent neighborhood.

It isn't difficult to imagine how impressive the complex once was. Two giant temple entrance gates, one to the east and one to the west, straddling the busy streets in the otherwise modern business district of Shiba once led directly to the temple grounds. When it was established in 1598 as the Tokugawa family temple, Zojo-ji with 50 sub-temples and 100 associated buildings, sprawled over 164 acres. The great gates are now each a good five-minute walk away from the current temple grounds. These days, while it is

still one of the biggest temples in Tokyo, only the main hall, three entrance gates, a few administrative buildings and the immediately surrounding grounds remain intact. The dominant feature of the landscape is neither the graceful temple gate nor the sloped roof of the main hall; it is the huge steel structure of Tokyo Tower, one foot of which appears to be growing out of the temple roof.

The imposing temple gates are visible from the exit at Daimon subway station. They still serve one of the purposes for which they were built: walking through them you can't help but feel a separation from the everyday world. Inside the temple grounds one finds few people, the sounds of traffic fade, and it is possible to feel a little peace.

On the way from the last gate to the main temple are a few noteworthy attractions. They include an 11-foot high bell dating from 1673 said to have been made from melted down metal hairpins donated by Tokugawa shogunate courtesans, a tree planted by U.S. President Ulysses S. Grant while on a visit in 1879 (One wonders how this tree survived the many fires and the bombing when all else was destroyed.), another tree planted by then U.S. Vice-President George Bush in 1982, and, an image of the Buddha's footprint carved in stone.

The large main temple, often the site of funerals of the rich and famous, is dark and fragrant inside, all elegant black and gold. The highly polished black lacquer floor reflects the golden Amida Buddha, the gold ceiling hangings and the pulpit from where the monks pray, creating the effect of a deep and mysterious pond.

To the right of the main hall is the Hall for the Safety of the Nation, a subsidiary building housing some treasures from the Tokugawa days, the 17th century. A sign posted outside reminds visitors to be especially careful during the bad luck ages — for men 25, 42 and 61 and for women 19, 33 and 61. During these years, the chance of accident, illness and just plain hard times are increased. The message is not just posted as a friendly reminder. These *yakudoshi*, or bad luck years, are a major source of income for temples around Japan. As a man or woman is about to turn one of these ages, he or she comes with the family for a special blessing from the monk in exchange for a donation of at least $100.

Just outside this hall are rows of *jizo*, or baby Buddha-like statues about two feet high, lined up on tiers, each with its own red crocheted cap, red cotton bib, and red and yellow plastic pinwheel spinning in the wind, creating a festive atmosphere. This gallery of 1,200 jizo is a charming and cheerful sight, until, that is, you learn that each one is here to honor and protect the spirit of a child or baby who has passed away. Suddenly the sight is poignant and sad.

On weekdays, the temple has few visitors. Today, there are a couple of business people perhaps taking a break between sales calls in the area and a pair of students stopping in to buy prayer boards, writing their plea for exam success on them and hanging them on the rack already filled with such requests. Also visiting are two European businessmen accompanied by a Japanese colleague apparently assigned to show them something of Tokyo during their stay. The Europeans are asking the usual tourist questions about the age of this or that building or object and become obviously annoyed when their host cannot answer to their satisfaction. They are less interested in the main temple when they learn that it only dates from 1972, the most recent time it was rebuilt. Their attention fades when they hear that though it was established in 1598, nothing that they see before them goes back that far.

Since its founding, the Temple has been destroyed and rebuilt several times. In recent history, it was deliberately burned down in 1868 by Shinto purists, rebuilt and then accidentally burned down again in 1909, and then after being rebuilt again was destroyed by bombs in 1945. Like Tokyo itself, Zojo-ji Temple keeps rising and the fact that the current building is not the original has little significance to local people. It is still Zojo-ji Temple regardless of the date on its cornerstone, its very presence and history reinforcing the Buddhist teaching of impermanence.

— S.F.M.

# Chronology

1457    Feudal lord Dokan Ota chooses the small fishing village of Edo as the site for his castle. This marks the founding of Edo/Tokyo.

1590    Ieyasu Tokugawa gains control of Edo and the surrounding provinces of eastern Japan.

1600    Tokugawa moves to Edo and begins to remodel the city by reclaiming marshland near the Bay, altering rivers and creating road networks. He builds an elaborate castle on the current site of Imperial Palace grounds.

1603    The Edo period begins as Tokugawa is named Shogun. Edo becomes the real capital of Japan.

1617    The Yoshiwara pleasure district is established.

1657    The Great Meireki Fire destroys nearly all of *shitamachi*, most of Edo castle, killing about 100,000 people. It is the most destructive of 1,800 fires that burned in the city during the Edo period.

1663    Shirokiya, Japan's first department store, opens in Nihonbashi.

1702    The 47 *ronin*, or masterless samurai, storm the household of a Shogunate official to revenge the killing of their lord. This true event will be recycled endlessly in drama, film, kabuki and television as Japan's greatest epic.

1720    The population reaches 1.3 million, making Edo the largest city in the world.

1853    The arrival in Tokyo Bay of American ships commanded by Commodore Matthew Perry, forces the opening of Japan to foreigners and mark the beginning of the end of the Edo period.

1868    The Meiji Era begins with the restoration of the Emperor as supreme ruler. Edo is renamed Tokyo, and an age of rapid modernization begins.

1872    Japan's first railroad connects Shimbashi with Yokohama.

1874    The Great Fire destroys much of the city, resulting in the rebuilding of the Ginza area in brick as opposed to the traditional wood.

1914    The Tokyo Station opens.

1923    The Great Kanto Earthquake. The quake, its aftershocks, fires and riots result in approximately 100,000 dead and 52,000 injured.

1926    The Showa Era begins; Hirohito becomes Emperor.

1927    The first subway, the Ginza line, opens.

1932    The city limits of Tokyo are redefined to include adjacent towns. By now Shinjuku and Shibuya have become major population and business centers.

1936    A bloody attempted coup fizzles after the Emperor refuses to support rebel army officers.

1943    The City of Tokyo is abolished and merged with rural counties to form *Tokyo To*, a prefectural-level unit of government that still exists.

1945    Americans bomb Tokyo during World War II. On the night of March 9-10, 700,000 bombs were dropped, destroying much of the city.

1952    The U.S. Occupation ends.

1958    The Tokyo Tower opens, one symbol of the rebuilding of Tokyo.

1964    The Tokyo Olympics trigger massive city planning projects and an opportunity to reintroduce modern Tokyo to the world.

1978    The New Tokyo International Airport opens in Narita, Chiba prefecture.

1986    Land prices start to soar, one of the indicators of the Bubble Era, which lasts until 1991.

1989    The *Heisei* era begins as Akihito becomes Emperor. The Mitsubishi Estate Co. buys Rockefeller Center in New York.

1991    The New City Hall opens in Shinjuku.

1995    A sarin gas attack in Tokyo subways kills 12 and injures thousands.

# Index

# About the Authors

Todd Crowell first lived in the Tokyo area as a child in the 1950s. He later returned in the late 1960s as a U.S. Air Force intelligence officer. He moved to Hong Kong in 1987 to work for *Asiaweek*, the regional English-language news magazine. He also contributes articles on Asia to the Boston-based *Christian Science Monitor*. His previous book, *Farewell, My Colony: Last Days in the Life of British Hong Kong*, was published by Asia 2000.

Stephanie Forman Morimura moved to Tokyo in 1980 from her home in Philadelphia. Originally intending to fulfil a two-year contract with the International Education Center, she met and married Kenji and made Tokyo her home. She served as Director of the Center for Japanese Studies and wrote a weekly column on cross-cultural communication for the mass circulation daily *Mainichi Shimbun* and a monthly column for the weekly *Business Computer News*. She currently divides her time between New York and Tokyo.

# Orchid Pavilion Books

Orchid Pavilion Books is the literary imprint of Asia 2000 Ltd., Hong Kong publishers of quality books since 1980. The imprint is inspired by the *Orchid Pavilion Preface*, a treatise on life penned by Wang Xizhi, China's most famous calligrapher.

To quote from *Behind the Brushstrokes*, an Asia 2000 book by Khoo Seow Haw and Nancy Penrose:

> By 352 A.D., Wang Zizhi was 50 years old, his reputation as a calligrapher was well established, and he had served as a court minister for many years. In the late spring of that year Wang Xizhi invited 41 calligraphers, poets, relatives and friends to accompany him on an outing to Lan Ting, the Orchid Pavilion, in the city of Shaoxing, Zhejiang province. It was the time of the year for the purification ceremony, when hands and bodies were cleansed with stream water to wash away any bad luck. The group of friends and scholars sat on each side of a flowing stream, and a little cup made out of a lotus leaf, full of wine, was floated down the stream. Whenever it floated in front of someone, that person was obliged to either compose a poem on the spot or to drink the wine as forfeit if he failed to come up with a poem.
>
> By the end of the day, 37 poems had been composed by 25 scholars. Wang Xizhi, as the head of this happy occasion, picked up a brush made out of rat whiskers and hairs and wrote on the spot the greatest masterpiece of Chinese calligraphy, the *Lan Ting Xu*, or the *Orchid Pavilion Preface*. Written on silk in the outstanding style of *Xing Shu* (Walking Style), the composition contains 28 vertical rows and 324 words. It is a philosophical discourse on the meaning of life. Wang Xizhi's calligraphy in this work is full of a natural energy, inspired by the happiness and grace of the moment, brimming with refinement and elegance. The *Orchid Pavilion Preface* became the greatest piece of *Xing Shu* and, although Wang Xizhi later tried more than 100 times to reproduce the work, he was never able to match the quality of the original.

# Quality Books

**ASIA 2000**

# From Asia 2000

## Fiction

| | |
|---|---|
| Dance with White Clouds | Goh Poh Seng |
| Lipstick and Other Stories | Alex Kuo |
| Chinese Opera | Alex Kuo |
| The Last Puppet Master | Stephen Rogers |
| Sergeant Dickinson | Jerome Gold |
| The Ghost Locust | Heather Stroud |
| Shanghai | Christopher New |
| A Change of Flag | Christopher New |
| The Chinese Box | Christopher New |
| Last Seen in Shanghai | Howard Turk |
| Cheung Chau Dog Fanciers' Society | Alan B Pierce |
| Riding a Tiger, The Self-Criticism of Arnold Fisher | Robert Abel |
| Childhood's Journey | Wu Tien-tze |
| Getting to Lamma | Jan Alexander |
| Chinese Walls | Xu Xi |
| Daughters of Hui | Xu Xi |
| Hong Kong Rose | Xu Xi |
| Temutma | Rebecca Bradley & Stewart Sloan |

## Poetry

| | |
|---|---|
| Round — Poems and Photographs of Asia | Barbara Baker & Madeleine Slavick |
| Traveling With a Bitter Melon | Leung Ping-kwan |
| Coming Ashore Far From Home | Peter Stambler |
| Salt | Mani Rao |
| The Last Beach | Mani Rao |
| Water Wood Pure Splendour | Agnes Lam |
| Woman to Woman | Agnes Lam |
| New Ends, Old Beginnings | Louise Ho |
| An Amorphous Melody — A Symphony in Verse | Kavita |

## *Order from* Asia 2000 Ltd

Fifth Floor, 31A Wyndham Street, Central, Hong Kong
Telephone: (852) 2530-1409; Fax: (852) 2526-1107
E-mail: sales@asia2000.com.hk; Website: http://www.asia2000.com.hk